# ONE PLUS ONE EQUALS ONE

# ONE PLUS ONE EQUALS ONE

## A CRYSTAL BOOK

A Division of CRYSTAL HORIZON INVESTMENTS GROUP
www.gideonadjei.com
Since 1999

EDITED BY
Professor Dominique Endrinal

CONSULTING EDITORS

Leon James, Ph.D.
Professor of Psychology
University of Hawaii, Honolulu

Harvey L. White, Ph.D.
President, American Society for Public Administration
Special Assistant to the Vice-President of Medical Affairs
Director, Center for Healthy Communities
University of South Alabama

Ed. McNack, Ed.D.
Asst. Dept Chair, Houston Community College System
Houston, Texas

Bob Richardson
Field Services Representative
FamilyLife, a Division of Campus Crusade for Christ
Frisco, Texas

Michael Bradley
Bible Knowledge Ministries
St. Charles, MO

Joe Ortega
Director
FIHNEC USA
International Director of Full Gospel Business Men's Fellowship International

Modesto (Moe) Rivera, Jr.
President, Full Gospel Business Men's Fellowship International, Humble Chapter
LTC, Field Artillery (Retired), U.S. Army
Professional Accountant/Houston Airport System

This book is the work of the author's personal experiences, opinions, travels, visions, interviews, and statement of facts or discovery from various sources. Any resemblance to other persons, living or dead, events, or locales is entirely coincidental. This book is sold with the understanding that neither the author nor the publisher is engaged in rendering any opinions or advice that may be construed as a substitute for independent professional advice.

The publisher and author disclaim any personal liability, directly or indirectly, for opinions presented herein. We have made every effort to ensure the accuracy and completeness of information contained in this book but assume no responsibility for errors, omissions, inaccuracies, or any inconsistencies herein. Any slights of people, publishers, books or organizations are coincidental. If you purchased this book without a cover, you should be aware that this book is stolen property. It was reported as "unsold and destroyed" to the publisher, and neither the author nor the publisher has received any payments for this "stripped book."

The cover format and design of this book are protected trade dresses and trademarks of Crystal Books, a division of Crystal Horizon Investments Group. For information, address: Crystal Books, P.O. Box 842061, Houston, Texas 77284-2061.

Cover design concept by Dr. Gideon Adjei. Graphic design by Trevor Piper. All rights reserved. No part of this book may be reproduced or transmitted in any form or by any means, electronic or mechanical, including photocopying, recording or by any information storage and retrieval system, without the written permission

of the publisher or author, except where permitted by law. For information, address
Crystal Books, Houston, Texas or

Website: www.gideonadjei.com
Email: adjei@gideonadjei.com or
denise@gideonadjei.com
Crystal Books is a "registered trademark" of Crystal Horizon Investments Group, and
the colophon is a trademark of Crystal Horizon Investments Group.
Library of Congress Registration Number TX u-331-335
ISBN 0-9715523-7-1
Printed in the United States of America 2007

This book is dedicated to families throughout the world.

## TABLE OF CONTENTS

| | | |
|---|---|---|
| CHAPTER 1 | Introduction | |
| CHAPTER 2 | What Motivated Me to Write This Book? | |
| CHAPTER 3 | The Plan | |
| CHAPTER 4 | Does Your Decision to Marry Fit into the Divine Plan? | |
| CHAPTER 5 | The Prohibitive Cost of Marital and Relationship Breakdown | |
| CHAPTER 6 | Menopause and Andropause | |
| CHAPTER 7 | Family Violence | |
| CHAPTER 8 | Promoting a Healthy Marital Relationship | |
| CHAPTER 9 | How to Strengthen Family Relationships | |
| CHAPTER 10 | Revelation of the Victorious Vision | |
| CHAPTER 11 | Proper Nutrition | |
| CHAPTER 12 | Positioning the Children of 21$^{st}$ Century Families for Success | |
| CHAPTER 13 | Additional Impediments to Victory | |
| CHAPTER 14 | Don't Turn Out the Lights, the Party Is Not Over for Victorious 21$^{st}$ Century Families | |

# ACKNOWLEDGMENTS

In a recent trip to Israel, I learned that the correct name of the Savior or Messiah is *Yahshua*. It means God's salvation. There are other variations of the same name, such as *Yeshua*, or *Yehoshua*. I have chosen to use Yahshua in this book instead of the transliterated and more widely known or English version, *Jesus*. It is to Him that I owe my deepest gratitude.

I would like to thank my wife, Denise for her love, support, encouragement, and critique of the manuscript. Sincere appreciation also goes to my children, Alvin and Vanessa Adjei for providing teenage insights during the preparation of the manuscript.

The author would specially like to recognize Dr. Leon James, Professor of Psychology, University of Hawaii; Dr. Harvey L. White, President-Elect, American Society of Public Administration; Dr. Ed. McNack, Dr. Bill Cotton, Mr. Michael Bradley, Bible Knowledge Ministries, Mr. Bob Richardson; Col. Moe Rivera and Mr. and Mrs. Joe Ortega for providing editorial reviews or praise for this work. Sincere thanks also go to Dr. Michael Lam and Bible.org of Dallas, Texas for permission to cite excerpts from their literary work.

The author is grateful to Professor Dominique Endrinal for his meticulous editing of the manuscript.

I am deeply indebted to Rev. W. Ed. Lockett, Senior Pastor, Metropolitan C.M.E. Church, Houston, Texas, and his Prayer Warriors-Peggy Robinson, Bertha Kelley, Kenneth and Michelle Mathis for their prayers and encouragement. Special thanks also go to Deloris Nsonamoah, Effie Doty, and Lana Van Marter, for their comments.

Finally, I would like to thank Claudia de Luna, Tomi Middleton, and Peggy Wendelken all at Houston Community College System, Town and Country campus for their invaluable perspectives on marriage in general.

# PREFACE

ONE PLUS ONE EQUALS ONE is written to provide guidance for 21$^{st}$ century families toward building strong marital and family relationships. This inspirational book is largely based on the Divine blueprint for marital and family units.

In order to promote a better appreciation for the success of the marital institution, certain key elements that must be understood by the marrying couple have been woven into three conceptual levels of unity in the marriage relationship.

These three levels provide an opportunity for the reader to examine behavior in the context of marriage by identifying the sub-components of gender habits in men and women within the three domains of behavior.

This powerful book is unique in many respects. In order to ensure marital success, the book provides additional factors that must be considered prior to making the decision to get married. For example, specific insights have been provided into how one must look before leaping into a marriage, and how to predict marital dissatisfaction.

Dr. Adjei discusses in detail, major elements, encompassing both physical and spiritual realms, that could crumble marital relations, and how to overcome them. Several elements set this set this book apart from others. For example, the author has included sections that provide both direct and indirect costs of marital breakdown at the government level. Furthermore, he has included a section on marital strife in the workplace, especially, the United States. This connotes the need for programs to strengthen marriages or at least make marriage conferences available for employees to attend. But there is more.

ONE PLUS ONE EQUALS ONE, additionally provides information on the cost of marital and family breakdown on our most precious resource- children of society.

Another unique attribute of this book is that it does not only identify family issues and problems. It gives the reader possible solutions to the challenges presented in this book. Beginning at the climax of the book, Dr. Adjei piques the reader's imagination with a strong "Revelation of the Victorious Vision!" This "Revelation" outlines, in a stepwise manner, the seven prerequisites for victory in the $21^{st}$ century, for building healthy marital and strong family relations.

Among other things, the book contains information on how to get back one with God. This information is supported by many Bible verses with emphasis on prayer and spiritual warfare; how to wait on answers from God; hindrances to prayer; proper equipment for spiritual warfare; standing on the promises of God; how to tap into God's blessings, and guarantees of Divine protection.

Invaluable information is provided on overcoming anger, anxiety, fear, depression, sadness, and stress; strengthening of family relationships; proper nutrition, self-control; maintaining control of the tongue, and money. Subsequently, the reader is taken to a different level of excitement by an imaginary journey that contained the 14 attributes that should be taught our children in order to position them for success.

This must-read book concludes with powerful examples from the Bible of those who did well even when they faced adversity. That means the problems faced by $21^{st}$ century families are not entirely new, and therefore they can be overcome if properly understood.

Welcome to the vision of ONE PLUS ONE EQUALS ONE!

Bob Richardson
Field Services Representative
FamilyLife
A Division of Campus Crusade for Christ
Frisco, Texas

## A REVIEW OF ONE PLUS ONE EQAUALS ONE

Dr. Gideon Adjei has written another book that is set within the intellectual premise that "the problems of humankind are rooted in spiritual sources." It enjoins us to "focus more on the spiritual rather than the physical realm" if we want to find "permanent solutions" to the problems of society and the world.

The key to these solutions lies in understanding and honoring the idea that marriage is a "Divine blueprint" for the perfect union between a man and a woman. Upon this unity rests the survival of society and the happiness of families. The love of married partners and their loyalty to one another is the basis for worshipping God. The oneness between a man and a woman can only be achieved in a marriage dedicated to God and sanctioned by God.

The battle for saving a marriage is a spiritual battle against "evil spirits" who play into and excite people's inherited tendencies towards selfishness and arrogance, pride and stubbornness. This kind of "spiritual warfare" produces in its wake conflict, disloyalty, mutual resentments, and ultimately, separation and divorce.

Dr. Adjei takes the position that maleness and femaleness are attributes of the body, not of the soul, and that the soul is genderless. However, an alternative view is that the body must reflect the mind, and this in turn reflects the soul. From the rational and scientific perspective, there must be unity and synergy within an individual's (a) soul, (b) mind or spirit, and (c) body. A female body is the direct result of a female mind or spirit, which in turn is the result of a female soul. However, since Scripture does not explicitly discuss the mental and spiritual anatomy of men and women, different interpretations have been given.

Dr. Gideon Adjei states that he is not a professional psychotherapist or counselor but a "modern day prophet" who has written this book by "divine inspiration" from a sense of Christian charity to aid those who are in mental pain due to marriage problems. He calls this book "the inspired word of God" who has "revealed mysteries to me in my dreams." The author "felt led by the Holy Spirit to write this book" and to use his 35 years of experience observing and interviewing family units.

It is important that partners acknowledge that marriage has a Divine purpose, which is to actualize at the human level the unity that exists in God Himself. The partners do God's will when they look upon mental intimacy between each other as representing that unity in God. In other words, husband and wife are to manage themselves in such a way as to achieve true mental intimacy with each other for the sake of the Lord whom they both wish to serve and love.

According to Dr. Adjei, "marriage is a major part of God's plan to bring redemption to the human race." By agreeing to treat their marriage as holy in God's purpose, husband and wife serve God and acquire the love and wisdom necessary to be an upright and supportive partner in marriage. The author says, "in a relationship of mutual commitment, leaving is the negative aspect, and cleaving is the positive." God's commandment in the Bible that the husband "cleaves" to his wife means that marriage "has priority over everything else including children, friends, career, hobbies and ministry."

This position is unusual. One can often hear today expressions by parents affirming that children come first, or their old parents come first, or that their work projects come first, etc. Nevertheless, Dr. Gideon Adjei takes up the position that nothing whatsoever should interfere with the mental intimacy and mutual loyalty and friendship of married partners. The conjugal mental unity of one man and his wife constitutes God's desire and plan to create a heaven on earth through such a marriage.

Communication between husband and wife is a key aspect of achieving mental intimacy and success in a marriage based on the acknowledgment of God's plan. The author explains three key aspects of this communication process – talking, listening, and caring. The process of *talking* with each other in God's presence establishes intimacy and friendship between husband and wife. According to Dr. Adjei, "one's mate should be his/her best friend." The process of *listening* to each other in God's presence is to be honest in one's appearance of availability. This requires a sincere and motivated effort to keep away the enemies of listening – preoccupation, daydreaming, self-involvement, lack of interest. The process of *caring* for each other in God's presence is to have the "genuine desire to understand the other person, to build areas of common ground, and to deepen the relationship."

The author discusses "the ideal husband" as performing the role of "head, God's representative authority" and therefore the husband is to take the initiative, leadership, and responsibility for the marriage relationship." The author does not make it clear specifically what consists of "initiative, leadership, and responsibility." The common interpretation of this Christian principle (e.g., Ephesians 5:21 cited by the author), is that the wife's religious duty is to agree to the husband's decision making regarding all family and marriage issues. However, I suggest that there are two opposite ways that a husband can perform this leadership responsibility, one being a good way, in accordance with God's plan, the opposite way being contrary to the mental intimacy and unity that is part of God's plan for every married couple.

The bad way of applying this principle of the husband being the "head" is to interpret it as giving the husband Divine warrant to exercise authority over the wife, who then becomes his obedient female servant, rather than his best friend. In fact, women tend to train themselves as they go through life to understand relationships and to look out for those they love and want to protect, especially their husbands. If the husband wants to become his wife's best friend, he has to use his leadership and decision making intelligence to manage his own behavior towards her in such a way as to become best friend in actual reality.

This cannot be achieved at all if the husband takes the point of view that he is the final authority the wife must respect whenever he makes a decision. It is not enough to say that the husband should also listen to his wife, but that in the end, the husband's decision must be the one that counts. The husband has no warrant to interpret being the head" as meaning his ultimate God-given authority over his wife. It is very important that Christian men do not fall into the trap of self-intelligence by which they give a self-serving interpretation of what it means to be the "head" of the marriage relationship.

The New Testament teaches that to be great in God's eyes or heaven, one should be great in serving the neighbor. From this principle, the husband is to serve his wife in such a way that he honors her insights, listens to her with a positive perspective, and refrains from exercising dominion over her by using the idea that he is the "head" and the "leader who makes the final decisions." The author emphasizes, "submission does not mean passivity or servility."

The author gives practical suggestions for how husbands are to build mental intimacy, unity, and friendship with their wife. These include being "sensitive to her emotional needs," retaining courtesy and good manners; hence, no angry outbursts, or walking out in anger, are allowed. One advice is given to both husband and wife: "Leave the weaknesses to the Lord and pray about them."

However, there is a bad way of performing this, and a good way. A wife for instance is very keen about her husband's appearance, clothes, or manner of speaking. She only wants the best for him when she tells him to change this or that in his habits. If she sees weaknesses in his habits, is she merely to pray about them?

Praying is good, but it is not enough, it seems to me. Instead the husband should be advised to listen to his wife when she tries to get him to change this or that habit that are not in order – like habits of cleanliness, or inappropriate verbal expressions and expletives, etc. When the husband is not in order, the wife can and should help him to get himself into order. However, she can do this only if he cooperates with her by listening to her, honoring her requests, and refraining from exercising authority over her.

The book addresses the important issue of how to prepare for the Christian marriage, starting with dating practices. Advice includes being friendly, warm, observant, and positive. "Be yourself" and "Have a clear profile of whom you really want." Moreover, "Do not be misled by love at first sight." A key element of this behavioral recipe: "Learn to place yourself under Divine order. He will guide your decisions and actions." There is more advice: commitment to the relationship, forging consensus agreement on issues like career, house, and children.

I think all this is good advice, to be sure, but at the same time, a key issue remains: How to get one to manage to perform this advice. In addition, what about the period of the struggle when a man does get angry and disrespectful, silent and withdrawn – what is the wife to do and how is she to handle this very common situation? It is to be hoped that Dr. Adjei will consider these specific practical issues in his next volume on this most important subject.

The book considers other marriage related issues and discusses them, as for instance, the causes and cost of divorce, both financial and psychological on the family and children. The author has advice on how to cope when couples have become a "blended family" with multiple parents and stepchildren involved in a variety of conflicts. The author discusses some "factors that crumble marital relationships" and these include abuse, infidelity, addictions, poor communication, and "spiritual factors" like occult practice, divination, transcendental mediation, and imaginary playmates.

The book has a chapter devoted to "Menopause and Andtropause." The reader is given a "brief lesson" discussing the physiology of menopause and related emotional and medical conditions. There is also a Chapter on "Family Violence." There is a Chapter on "How to Strengthen Family Relationships" which lists and explains the characteristics of "strong families"

There is a relatively long chapter on the author's vision of the future. It is titled "Revelation of the Victorious Vision." The author relies here on his special enlightenment in the area of "spiritual warfare." We are warned that "the devil is a formidable adversary" showing up in people's lives in the form of "depression, anger, jealousy, or stress." These are our "oppressors" and the author wants us to be prepared for battling them with appropriate weapons of truth from the Word of God, which is the Sword of the Spirit.

The author has dozens of references to passages in the New Testament that provide us with the Scriptural ideas of opposition to our servitude to the devil. The reader is provided with hundreds of pieces of advice or principles of behavior and attitude that oppose our slavish nature and help us to gain victory over our baser nature that has no place in heaven.

There is even an extensive discussion of what constitutes a healthy nutrition for those who want to keep themselves in the order of heaven. There is a discussion on how to raise children and what benefits children. The final chapter, the fourteenth, is devoted to the author's vision of "victorious $21^{st}$ century families" expressed in the form of a listing of passages in the Bible that depict exemplar marriage and family unity.

ONE PLUS ONE EQUALS ONE is a memorable book that gives Christian readers a better understanding of the process of marriage as a Divine plan for redemption. It provides a network of Biblical passages in which God reveals and describes His plan for the marriage process by which a husband and a wife cleave to each other in the presence of God. Advice is given on what the husband can do, and what the wife can do, to develop mental intimacy that forms a spiritual bond of friendship and interdependence.

Leon James, Ph.D.<br>
Professor of Psychology<br>
University of Hawaii

## RIGOR AND RELEVANCE OF
## ONE PLUS ONE EQUALS ONE

"This is one solid piece of anointed work by Dr. Adjei. I would highly recommend this book to people who are not only looking to get married, but to people who are already married. It is never too late to improve the quality of one's marriage.

All of the solid biblical truths given in this book is backed up from the light of Scripture. Dr. Adjei not only covers the basics of the actual personal relationship that should be established between a loving husband and wife. He also incorporates additional topics not usually discussed in other books on this particular subject matter. For example, he discusses the impacts of spiritual warfare, proper nutrition, menopause and andropause on marital relations. He believes a lack of understanding of these subject areas could get married couples into serious trouble, if not properly handled.

The title of this book, "One Plus One Equals One," says it all. The Bible tells us that two people become one flesh when united by marriage. However, though most people already know this, Dr. Adjei goes into great detail as to what this one-flesh union really means and how to actually help deepen this very special spiritual union between a married couple and the Lord.

The only way any marriage union can survive in this present day and age is if it is totally grounded in the Lord and His Word. Dr. Adjei gives the reader all of the appropriate verses from the Bible and their correct interpretation to help establish and ground the marriage union in the Lord. Again, I cannot recommend this book highly enough to anyone who is either looking to get married or to anyone who is already in a marriage union. It is never to late to be able to turn one's marriage around. The secrets of the plan contained in this book will help you do this successfully."

Michael Bradley<br>
Bible Knowledge Ministries<br>
St. Charles, MO

## THE VALUE OF
## ONE PLUS ONE EQUALS ONE
## TO 21st CENTURY FAMILIES

ONE PLUS ONE EQUALS ONE is a majestically well thought out, analyzed and spiritually inspired family manuscript. This elaborate document draws in the 21$^{st}$ Century reader through fourteen chapters of solid statistical data and advice that depict the main causes of the breakdown of the universal family nucleus.

On the bright side, it counteracts such break down with Godly-based biblical principles, doctrine and precepts. In addition, it points out a nutritional plan that, if followed by the reader, will definitely increase the quantity and quality of life.

Dr. Gideon Adjei sincerely draws out a solid course of action that will guide the reader to a happy successful life. I thank the Lord for the author. During the relatively short time that I have known Dr. Adjei, I perceive him as a gifted author, teacher, minister, prophet and Godly man in the faith. He has a beautiful family and it is not by coincidence since it involves mentoring and what the military calls, "Leading by Example."

Keep the faith: I am sure the Lord Yahweh Adonai will say, "Son, well done."

Modesto (Moe) Rivera, Jr.
LTC, Field Artillery (Retired), U.S. Army/President, Full Gospel Business Men's Fellowship International,
Humble Branch, Houston, Texas

OTHER BOOKS BY
Dr. Gideon Adjei


BLACK ICE: A Vision for Victory
DARKER SHADES OF LIGHT


Pending Books
THE CRYSTAL HORIZON
TEARS FROM AN INNOCENT HEART
VANESSA's SWORD
HOPE

## ADDITIONAL PRAISE FOR
## ONE PLUS ONE EQUALS ONE

Rev. Dr. Adjei has prepared an excellent document for understanding the issues that challenge $21^{st}$ century families globally. He expounds on issues of the family, marriage, divorce, prayer, God, and the Holy Spirit. He has done an excellent job in connecting the relationship of God and family problems confronting the world in the $21^{st}$ century. I found it to be inspirational, factual, informative, and well-balanced. Anyone who reads this book will get a better appreciation for the Divine blueprint for marriage.

Each chapter of the book echoes a specific theme on family issues of the $21^{st}$ century. Collectively all the chapters cohere well and provide standards, documentation, and pertinent information regarding the Divine blueprint for marriage. Scriptural references make this book an excellent reinforcing commitment to God, family, marriage, and society.

A man of many talents, Dr. Adjei allows the reader to know that this book was written under divine inspiration. He combines divine, scientific, and philosophical concepts to motivate the reader to overcome divisive family issues. Dr. Adjei has provided an in depth coverage of family relationship, marriage, unwed mothers, low income married couples, and the importance of saving and strengthening marital and family relationships. This is a must read for all families.

Dr. Eddie C. McNack<br>
Professor & Asst. Dept Chair<br>
Houston Community College System<br>
Houston, Texas

We truly believe this book was sent from above for such a time as this. In a fascinating manner, the author provides invaluable information that has direct relevance to family matters of the present age. The reader's attention is captivated by the insightful biblical advice against the background of hope, and encouraging references from the Scriptures. We were touched by the awesome power of the author's personal testimonies. They underscore the practicality and reality of the concepts presented in this book. The author strengthened our hope and faith in God by the confirmation that, with God on our side, family problems are not entirely new and can be overcome. This is necessary read book for families everywhere. We recommend ONE PLUS ONE EQUALS ONE to be used as a teaching tool for group studies on how to attain successful marital relations. It impressed upon our mind the need for guidance and focused direction in the quest for married couples to truly attain oneness in their relationship. We were excited and greatly blessed by it.

Joe and Rosa Ortega<br>
Directors<br>
FIHNEC USA/International Directors, Full<br>
Gospel Business Men's Fellowship International

It is refreshing to see Dr. Adjei's efforts to refocus 21st century families' attention from the divisions that cause sensationalism, to the unifying aspects of creating family unity and strength by incorporating biblical principles to maintaining strong family relations and health.

William Cotton, D.C., C.C.S.P.<br>
Houston Community College System<br>
Houston, Texas

This is certainly a rare, and excellent document. It contains lots of information about every aspect of "married and family life!" I strongly recommend it for married or soon to be married people.

Mrs. Deloris Nsonamoah, M.S.<br>
Business Technology Instructor<br>
Houston Community College System<br>
Houston, Texas

ONE PLUS ONE EQUALS ONE is a fantastic book. It has positive information for 21st century families, globally. Those who are already in a married relationship, as well as anyone seriously considering marriage should read it. This book empowers the reader to know and lay the groundwork for a wholesome, happy family.

Effie Doty, B.A.<br>
Retired School Teacher<br>
Houston, Texas

ONE PLUS ONE EQUALS ONE is a truly thought-provoking book. The pages burst with relevant information, sagacious advice, and helpful illustrations. This future classic is just what the doctor ordered for the youth of my generation concerning marriage and family relationships.

Vanessa Adjei<br>
Langham Creek High School<br>
Houston, Texas

A child of Light, a Minister of Yahshua (Jesus Christ), Rev. Dr. Adjei has combined his personal experience, training, and vocation in expressing timeless insights and wisdom in this book - ONE PLUS ONE EQUALS ONE. Each family united by God should benefit from its guidance.

Lana Van Marter, M.A, M.B.A.<br>
Former Diplomat, Republic of the Philippines

ONE PLUS ONE EQUALS ONE is masterfully written. This enlightening book uniquely combines a spiritual, physiological, and psychological perspective to encourage and inform the reader. Rev. Dr. Adjei guides the reader in understanding the devastation of divorce especially on children, and empowers the reader to rise above the challenges that marriage brings. This is a must read book for anyone thinking about marriage.

Alvin Adjei<br>
Student<br>
University of Notre Dame<br>
Notre Dame, Indiana

## ABOUT THE AUTHOR

Favor is what happens when preparation meets opportunity. God has prepared Reverend Dr. Gideon Adjei for such a time as this to help save the most important of all social institutions-The Family!

It was merely through the guidance of the Holy Spirit that in this book, ONE PLUS ONE EQUALS ONE, Reverend Adjei was able to unfold God's Divine plan to fight against the devastating upsurge of family dissolution that crosses boundaries of castes, races, and income-levels.

Since families are painfully cognizant that something is missing in the home, he challenges them to devote their spiritual and intellectual abilities totally to God's Divine order for the Family. ONE PLUS ONE EQUALS ONE will definitely earn the respect of millions of scholars and fascinate the interest of general readers.

The Reverend Dr. Gideon Adjei is a prophet and crusader for God. His abilities, however, scope far beyond the pulpit, as he has become an international evangelist, agog speaker and acclaimed writer. He brings to his writing an extraordinarily diverse background and a wide range of interest academically and spiritually.

He is the author of *Darker Shades of Light, Black Ice, Vanessa's Sword, Hope, The Crystal Horizon, and Tears from an Innocent Heart.* He has received extensive training at Texas A&M University, Oklahoma State University, The University of Arizona, The University of Houston, and a certificate from the University of London.

Rev. Dr. Adjei lives in Houston, Texas with his wife, Denise and children.

Denise Adjei, M.S., CPM

# CHAPTER I

## Introduction

I have come to discover that most of the problems of humankind are rooted in spiritual sources. I believe in order to find permanent solutions to our problems; humankind must focus more on the spiritual rather than the physical realm.

This is a key element of ONE PLUS ONE EQUALS ONE. It is an inspirational plan given to me directly from God for the strengthening of families globally. It is my hope and prayer that families throughout the world will be encouraged to take a closer look at their marital and family relationship issues from God's perspectives rather than the precepts of humankind.

In other words, humankind must learn to, "Render unto Caesar the things that are Caesar's, and unto God the things that are God's." We can do so by following the Divine blueprint for marriage presented herein.

The Divine blueprint for marriage is firmly rooted in spiritual principles. It prescribes leaving, cleaving, and becoming as One with our spouse. However, it also implies that we strive to ultimately become the faithful spouse of our inner-self, and God Himself. Nevertheless, it does not stop there. It provides additional specific guidelines not only for the married couple but for the entire family unit, as follows:

- The husband is head of the wife. This in no way implies that one is inferior to the other.
- A husband must love his wife. A man who loves his wife loves himself.
- Children must obey their parents.
- Fathers must not provoke their children to wrath but bring them up in the nurture and admonition of God.

In essence, a healthy marriage is tantamount to the narrow rather than the broad gate through which we enter the Kingdom, and become One with God.

One might ask, "How can two individuals become one flesh?" There is One God. He manifests Himself as God the Father, God the Son, and God the Holy Spirit. Yet, He is One and the same. God is Light. Yet visible light has seven components, as depicted in the colors of the rainbow. One sperm cell can fertilize a single egg giving rise to an individual organism. Similarly, multiple eggs can be fertilized by multiple sperm cells, leading to multiple babies. Whether a single baby is born or multiple babies are born, these developments constitute a single pregnancy.

One might ask the same question in a different way, "Can two individuals of the opposite sex become one flesh?" The resounding answer is, "Yes". The simplest level of organization of living things is the chemical level. At this level are the atoms that react with each other to form molecules, compounds, and etc.

Elementary Chemistry teaches that, while there are other sub-atomic particles, the two key factors involved in an atom's electrical properties are its electrons and protons. The number of protons is always equal to the number of electrons. The proton carries a positive charge, while the electron carries a negative charge. Because the neutron carries no charge, the positive and negative charges cancel out making one atom electrically neutral .

If the desire of marriage is to be as one in accordance with the Divine blueprint for marriage, then this book is for you.

The principles and suggestions presented in this book should help get to that point. When you and your spouse become convinced you have attained Oneness, that is, the two of you have become physically and mentally of one mind, then the seven spiritual centers within each begin to move in harmony and balance. Relationships at this stage cannot usually be broken from without the marriage.

You would have set the stage in motion for the biblical reality of one flesh to be manifested in your lives. The exchange of bodily fluids through "knowing your wife" in the biblical sense, is the fundamental passageway by which two physical bodies become bonded. This is the genesis of the process of becoming one flesh.

Lionel Ritchie and Diana Ross wrote and sang a hit song entitled, "Endless Love" several years ago. The central theme of their lyrics was that in order to become one flesh, the individual spouses must see themselves as the left and right halves of the human heart. Each beats in total and complete harmony with the other half.

Remember that this spiritual union can only be brought about through the power of God. So powerful and serious is this union that according to Yahshua (Jesus), either spouse who looks at someone else outside the marriage with lustful eyes is considered to have committed an act of adultery in the eyes of God (Matt. 5:28).

Clearly, the physical attractions and desires for the opposite sex transcend biological needs. These urges lie deep in the soul of humankind. They are manifestations of our inner efforts to reestablish who we really are. Its ultimate goal is to restore one's state of oneness in the physical world of divided reality.

Thus, careful choice, commitment, truthfulness in mate selection is imperative to avoid being 'unequally yoked.' Oneness requires that both spouses be bonded both physically, mentally, and spiritually. But that is not all. The couple must purge or shield themselves from defilements of past sexual relations outside their marriage.

I Cor. 6: 15-20 admonishes us that a spouse who is connected to some other person outside the marriage is not a desirable spouse. When an individual has sex with someone, that individual is, in essence, sexually tied with everyone the person had sex with.

Such esoteric factors continue to be a secondary presence throughout the relationship in view (16). Consequently, one could expect to be unable to rise above the level of one's many sexual partners who anchor their bodies and minds to the things of this world.

That was depicted in a story of the Samaritan woman at the well recorded in John 4: 18. During that encounter, Yahshua being God-man, saw the stream of vital force from five different men upon which their thoughts and level of being was entering the Samaritan woman. Because of the 'polluted environment' thus created, she had difficulty maintaining a healthy relationship.

The story of the "Prodigal Son," told by Yahshua, could be related to a lack of commitment in a family or marital relationship. The prodigal son had no commitment to his father. He prematurely asked for and received his portion of inheritance. Subsequently, he went to a far country. There, he squandered his earthly possessions with riotous living, and on harlots. Ultimately, he reduced himself to less than a pauper.

This is the path on which we tread without commitment in a marital relationship. Sooner or later we find ourselves seduced and reduced to sub-human poverty by the 'citizens of a far country of extra-marital relationships.' We may even stand the risk of shortening our lives because our vital spirit life-force and power of mind are drained, exposing us to the ills of this divided world of sensuality and materialism.

To ensure we do end up on this dismal path, we must learn to present our bodies as 'broken and contrite hearts' that would not be despised by God. Broken and contrite hearts tend to create a revival of the Holy Spirit within us. That would help us grow and nurture our family and marriage relationship to bear fruit, some thirty, sixty or one hundred fold.

If we choose to live outside the Divine blueprint for marriage. We run the risk of engaging in activities that might expose us to very costly spiritual battles. We open the flood gates in the spiritual realm that unleash certain strongholds to cause interferences in our marriage or family relationship.

Once such a spiritual battlefield is established, the couple can expect a complex, protracted, and sustained spiritual warfare. Such battles are not easy to win. Evil spirits do not usually operate alone. They wage war in bands and in concert with a host of other forces, as described in subsequent sections of this book.

Because of the foregoing reasons, great pains have been taken to provide all possible guidance to the reader so as to stay on the path prescribed in the Divine blueprint for marriage. Make no mistake about it. In order for us to be successful in our marital or family relationship, we must have God on our side. Unfortunately, some of us set the stage for trouble when we lose focus on our spirituality.

Naturally, people look upon themselves and each other in terms of their gender, race, gene pool, cultural or national origins. However, these perceptions do not reflect our true state of being.

Scripture teaches that humankind is composed of body, soul and spirit. The body is comprised of the elements. It functions in conformance to known and possibly not yet understood principles of physics and chemistry. .It is both temporary, and separable from spirit and soul. The body is susceptible to disease and death. It is recognized as the seat of the senses-the mechanism through which the spirit and soul attain world-consciousness. The term 'soul' implies self-conscious life. The human soul is the seat of emotions, desires, and affections. Finally, spirit is the component of the human that 'knows'. The spirit allies the human being to the spiritual creation. It imparts God-consciousness. The spirit and soul are permanent.

The physical body 'houses' the soul during its sojourn here on earth. The soul dwells in a realm where the forces of mind exist in harmony. It is neither male nor female. The soul is aware of its permanent residence in the spiritual realm. There is no such thing as a black, white, brown, red or yellow soul. Similarly, there can be no male or female soul.

The analogy of a soul residing in a physical body is equivalent to an ambassador of one country residing in a host country. During his or her sojourn, and tenure in the host country, the ambassador develops an intimate relationship with the leadership and people of the host country.

Yet, the laws of the host country do not govern the ambassador. Neither does he or she participate in the governance or political process of the host country. The Ambassador may be considered a traitor or spy if caught meddling in the internal affairs of the host country.

Should relations turn sour between the host and home country, the Ambassador may be recalled by his or her own country's President, who appointed the Ambassador, in the first place.

The soul resides in the physical body for a purpose and ordained duration of time within God's master plan. Should the body become incapacitated and lose its *will* to remain viable, God may recall the soul to its heavenly home.

At that point, the soul separates from the body. It is distilled into a pure state by removal of all human and earthly 'blemishes' before returning to its permanent home, where there is no respecter of persons. Truly, none but the righteous shall see God! Variations of these stages of transfigurations are known by different names such as astral body, rainbow body, body of pure bliss, spirit beings, heavenly body, or new body.

The mind provides an awareness of consciousness or self. It is the main point of contact or communication with God. Thus, it becomes a major battleground for most spiritual warfare. Since the living soul is interactive with its other components of the body, human problems or their solutions cannot be limited only to its temporary component individuals.

Humankind has gone round in circles with the application of such temporary, quick-fix solutions to problems of marital relation. Much of these carnal solutions never seem to work permanently. That is because we are looking for such solution in all the wrong places.

After all is said and done, and you have to take stock of your life here on earth, what legacy would you like to leave behind? Would you like to leave behind a legacy characterized by a track record of poor judgment, mistakes, instability, divorce, child abuse, crime, family violence, or would you rather leave behind a solidly impeccable record of love, happiness, stable marital relation, and a strong family. If you desire the latter, then I urge you to read on.

# CHAPTER 2

## What Motivated Me to Write This Book?

Dear Reader: Do not read this book with a preconceived notion or with the attitude that "all books on the family or marriage are the same, anyway." Because they are not, and I would urge you to be patient as you read this book with an open mind. Then, and only then will you begin to understand the real nature of the issues that affect the institution of marriage and the family structure as a whole.

A lot of family therapists, counselors, and psychotherapists mean well. They use the most current techniques known to humankind to help their clients. Nevertheless some of the assumptions they make in their diagnostic techniques are esoteric to the Divine purpose of marriage and the family unit. Therefore, it is likely that the reader would find points of departure from what someone else might have told them. This book was divinely inspired and rooted in spiritual principles. I am deeply convinced that it will point you in the right direction to a successful marriage and happier family relationship if you follow the principles outlined in it.

Some of the things I will narrate are thought-provoking. I intended for them to get your attention, cause you to step back, and think deeper about love, happiness, marriage, family, and relationships.

All living beings tend to have an affinity, attraction, or love for each other. This complex phenomenon is universal. That does not mean tensions do not arise among and between the various species of the world for territorialism. We come together to celebrate or to mourn.

We are happy when good things happen to us and to members of our families. We are sad when bad things happen to our loved ones, our neighbors, or sometimes us.

There are several million species of organisms on earth, yet there seems to be unity in this great diversity, even among members of the same species. There is strength in diversity. Look into the skies at dawn or dusk to admire how colorful nature is.

Take a close look at all the living things of the world, and you will find a colorful perfection in them. Even some of the inanimate things of the world are colorful. For example, several colorful soils abound on earth.

I know there are a few smart readers who might be wondering, "What about pure air and water?" Brilliant, very brilliant! These colorless components of the biosphere reflect, diffract, or allow the beauty of the nature to be expressed in them. Similarly, they may manifest their ultimate function and usefulness in the beautiful coloration of nature.

I am talking about the rainbow in the sky, the blue or greenish waters of the rivers and of the seas. I am talking about the transportation of oxygen in red blood, the use of oxygen in the green pigment, chlorophyll to produce energy molecules that sustain life on earth.

Scientists have tried to explain this phenomenon. For example, it has been established that all living beings are composed of cells, have a universal genetic code, and use the same twenty amino acids to make proteins. At the pinnacle of creation is mankind. The strength in diversity, even among the various ethnic groups of the world, is manifested as an interwoven cord of love, friendship, happiness, and value within and among all families of the world.

There are several good families in the world. However, the innate homeostatic cord of love, friendship, happiness, and value has steadily and spontaneously been disrupted or weakened by many factors. We now find ourselves existing in a 'troubled' world. These troubles infest our spiritual, physical, social, financial, occupational, and emotional well-being.

A review of available information on marriage and relationship breakdown throughout the world suggests something is wrong. One can go back in time to available records and find alarming breakdowns of the 'family unit.'

Recent debates on the definition or redefinition of 'marriage', domestic violence, abductions, and dismal events of that nature, might lead one to a very rude awakening that both 'marriage', and the 'family unit', is poorly understood. Yet, 'families' form the bulwark of nations. There seems to be a great distance between the current status of strength within a given family and where they would like to be. Regardless of the geographical location, it takes hard work to make a successful family. Those who choose to invest in strengthening, creating, maintaining, or improving their family relationship will ultimately reap benefits.

The great Chinese philosopher, Lao Tsu, said, "A journey of 1000 miles must begin with a single step." Let me extend this wise concept. Progressive and strong families must have dreams and visions of their future. Their dreams must be big but realistic. In order to achieve those dreams together with love, joy, friendship, happiness, and value, one needs to cultivate humility, endurance, perseverance, commitment, and patience.

These qualities provide the initial energy required for the first single step to maintain the homeostatic balance of the innate cord that holds families together. I believe there is worldwide recognition of the importance of improving family life.

Despite the work of sociologists, family therapists, marriage counselors, voluminous publications, past relational experiences, existing judicial definitions and rulings, religious texts and teachings, and all other information available to humankind in this area, it seems additional work is needed to explain the Divine plan for marriage and the family unit.

Several artists have written and made millions of dollars on love songs. Humankind continues to reach out for something to fill an inner void from within. For example, The Reverend Al Green thrilled audiences with his hit songs, "Let's Stay Together, Love and Happiness, Let's Get Married Today." On the other hand, Tina Turner captivated many with her hit song, "What's Love Got to Do with it."

The lyrics of both songs suggest there is something wrong with our concepts, and perspectives about marital and family relationships.

Many people live in pain and agony because of relationship problems. Granted, of course, that some relationships terminate amicably. By far, most breakups are hostile. A couple that at one time saw themselves as inseparable eventually become bitter enemies on opposite sides of a judge's bench in family courts.

Some people have committed suicide because of relationship breakdown. Teenage boys impregnate mature adult females. Husbands who once promised to love their spouses till 'death do us part' have petitioned courts to pull life support systems from their comatose spouses. People, including married members of the clergy, are having extra-marital relations with the same or opposite sex.

I wrote this book because I wanted to make a difference in the lives of families throughout the world. There are too many marital and relationship breakdowns. The family unit is crumbling at an alarming rate. I was convinced it was about time to provide a book written in plain language that would point humankind in the right direction concerning these matters. For over 2000 years, we have been exposed to the formula for a successful marriage and strong relationships in the Bible. However, most people never pay much attention to that.

I agree with the apostle Paul in the New Testament. The majority of people who truly believe in God should be 'teachers' by now. However, for various reasons, most of us "have need that one teaches us again which be the first principles of the oracles of God; and are become such as have need of milk, and not of strong meat. For every one that uses milk is unskillful in the word of righteousness: for he is a babe. But strong meat belongs to them that are full of age, even those who by reason of use have their senses exercised to discern both good and evil."

I am a Christian, and the Bible is the sole guide and inspiration for my writings. This book, however, is meant to provide a victorious vision for all of God's children, regardless of their geographic, religious or ethnic origin.

Let me restate that I feel inspired to help families build strong, successful relationships within the divine realm of marriage and family because 'for this reason shall a man leave his father, and his mother, and shall cleave unto his wife, and they shall be one flesh.'

## Basis of my authority

I am not a trained psychotherapist, family counselor or sociologist. I am an evangelist, scientist, philosopher, educator, businessman, and descendant of the Biblical patriarch, Moses, who loves God. I am an observer of people, and nature. I also consider myself a modern-day prophet.

Just like my 'mentors' in the Scriptures, God reveals mysteries to me in my dreams. I consider this book an inspired work of God. I would like to encourage people throughout the world to know that He still uses ordinary people to reach out to all His children, just as He did in days of old.

Again, I would like to reiterate my conviction that most of the problems of humankind originate from the spiritual rather than the physical realm. Consequently, mankind must seek spiritual rather than physical answers to correct such problems.

I know that not everyone is spiritual. I also understand, as a scientist, that many people will only conceptualize and appreciate things when presented to them in the context of known chemical and physical laws.

My real interest in understanding family relationships grew after the death of my mother, Mary Augustina Adjei, in 1995. She spent most of her life doing all she could to keep our family strong, and happy. And after my father also did pass away in 2000, the glue that held the children together eroded.

As a so-called 'Mama's Boy' then I felt the loss of both of our parents probably to a greater degree than my other siblings. At the time my mother passed, I was a single parent raising my two children, Alvin and Vanessa. I had come through a near-death experience brought about by an arranged marriage that turned sour. I struggled with that pain, in addition to the loss of my parents. I felt a great vacuum within me. A void as deep as the prophetic abyss.

Suddenly, there was no one to encourage and motivate me. All my siblings gravitated toward their spouses and children. The family values that once held our extended family together began to dismantle.

I have made many mistakes in my life. Yet, God has chosen, molded, and is using me for the expansion of His Kingdom. I know the God who has called me. He can and will use you for His purpose, if you humble yourself before Him. There are no issues in your marriage or family relationship too large for Him to help you surmount. The above opens entire volumes of transcendental and enigmatic mysteries beyond the scope of this book.

Come with me on an imaginary 35-year journey in time and space. Incidents and observations influenced me to write this book. Some of those incidents might be commonplace to you. Others might be awkward, pointed, pungent and unsuspecting to others. Be that as it may, I now believe they were part of God's master plan, to better prepare me to write this book. The journey begins.

While a doctoral student at the University of Arizona, I walked from the men's dorm to class. I was financially broke I could not afford a car. At approximately 7:40 each weekday morning, I saw a nicely dressed middle-aged woman who usually wore pearls. She dropped off on time her partially paralyzed husband who worked in the administration building of that university.

It appeared her husband had suffered a stroke or some other neurological trauma. However, he was usually dressed in a clean, crisp white shirt, tie, and slacks.

After parking, she pulled out her husband's wheelchair, and wheeled him into the administration building. I often asked myself, as pretty as that woman was, why would she be so devoted to someone who was unable to fulfill her major emotional needs compared to others she could have had?

One day the Holy Spirit gave me the answer to that question. She married him for love, "for better or worse until death do us part." That was my first real insight into love between married people. I then realized how childish I was.

I know you might be wondering whether I observed a loving relationship between my parents. Yes, my parents were married for over 60 years. It takes a lot of love to stay together for 60 years. But, you see, most Africans did not express love the way I now understand it.

In most African countries, grownups did not usually express their love for each other openly. They expressed or discussed it in the privacy of their bedroom or among other adults only. Therefore, I really did not quite have a good grasp of it. Yes, I had dated a few times in high school. Nevertheless, whatever observations about relationships I made were picked up from my friends who did not know any better about the true meaning of love than I did.

Of course, I should have known better. My older brother, who is an ordained Minister of the Gospels, and who overseas more than 400 churches in Ghana, is a cripple, not by birth but through medical malpractice. He was married, and had three children. For some reason, I thought about his circumstances differently from the paralyzed man at the University of Arizona. I could blame the devil for 'blinding my eyes' to that fact.

By the same token, I was confounded by a contradictory and strange affair that brewed between a former roommate of mine, much younger than I, and the wife of one of the professors in his department. Secret love affairs between married people have always frightened me. I knew it was wrong, and expected an angel of destruction to strike those who engaged in such adulterous relationships. I moved out of the dorm into an apartment off campus out of fear that something bad might happen to them, and I did not wish to be caught in the middle of it.

An additional experience that shaped my thinking regarding marriage and family relationships was an incident that occurred in San Antonio, Texas, in the early 1970s. An established African American medical doctor had marital problems with his wife. One day he decided to end it all by killing his entire family. He shot and killed his wife and children and finally himself.

Fortunately or unfortunately, his bullet crippled one of his daughters. Another one of his daughters escaped the gruesome ordeal. They were the most beautiful women you have ever seen in San Antonio. The one who missed the bullet married a medical student from my native home. Her sister who was crippled by the bullet was the bride's maid. I learned about their family circumstances during the wedding preparations.

I asked myself, "What goes through the mind of a successful person to want to destroy his entire family because of marital difficulties? Were there no available resources, family members, religious organizations, or support groups, to help rectify that situation? Did the person consider those issues too great for God to handle?"

One only needs to listen to the news on T.V. in order to hear horrific stories about children of divorced parents. No matter how nice people try to paint it, there is no such thing as reduced pain and anger in such children. This particular topic is covered in a subsequent chapter of this book. I will, therefore, defer further expansion on it at this time.

Even though the Scriptures remain the primary source of guidance and inspiration to the faithful, there remain large segments of people who belong to different faiths, people who do not belong to organized religious organizations, or much less read the bible. I have heard many true stories of infidelity, child abuse, rape, and other horrific incidents involving televangelists, local pastors, prominent politicians, and polygamous relationships among religious sects in many parts of the world.

As prayer director for a nationally known organization devoted to saving family relationships, I get the opportunity to share real life marital, and other relationship problems at conference settings. The high incidents of incest, especially here in the United States, convinced me of the lack of understanding and misinterpretation of Divine blueprint for marriage and family institution.

Consequently, I felt led of the Holy Spirit to write this book in plain language to make a difference in the lives of people. Professionals in the field of marital or family counseling, and religious leaders and support groups have done, and continue to do their best to alleviate the pain and save marital and family relationships. I have respect for the dedication of such professionals. However, the incidences of such breakdowns remain high.

I must admit I have little faith in some of the principles, assumptions, and presumptions under which some of these professionals operate. Textbook logic has not always correlated well with human issues. Those who have sought professional help seem to get temporary relief. However, the situations persist.

There was a classic example of a well-respected family therapist in a west Texas town. He had a nice big house, expensive vehicles, and all that was associated with status symbol. During the course of his marriage, it became evident his wife had sexual relations with a utility technician. His usual counseling methodologies did not help.

By virtue of the doctor's prominence, he was able to demand the repair technician be transferred to another town. Well, did that save his marriage? Your guess is as good as mine.

Finally, I have often wondered why certain nice looking people end up with unattractive mates. Someone once told me it was for his or her peace of mind. I have also heard that they find an inner beauty of their mates. I always have been of the opinion that a man should be entitled to a very attractive mate. I was curious to learn what was different about so-called 'pretty woman.'

I went through great lengths to date a very attracted young woman, who was known to date only professional football and basketball players. I was a government worker with meager income compared to that of professional athletes. What I discovered amazed me. It changed my thinking about the definition of an 'attractive woman' and outside beauty.

In that regard, I drew upon my own experiences and observations, conducted interviews with different people who were married for at least 35 years, reviewed available literature, and asked the Holy Spirit to guide me as I wrote this book.

I invite you to come with me on this spiritual journey into the world of marriage, as we explore victorious visions for the 21$^{st}$ Century Family.

Against this background, let us take a closer look at the Divine blueprint for marriage and family unit on the following sections of this book. Next, I will examine the track record of humankind in these two areas. Hopefully, we can begin to see a beacon of

victorious light at the end of the stark darkness that has characterized marriage and the family unit.

# CHAPTER 3

## The Plan

**Marriage**

A brief history on marriage has been presented elsewhere (37). Apparently, different cultures have different conceptions of marriage. For example, some marriages are arranged, others are considered either temporary or permanent. In other instances, the legal age for marriage is not clearly defined (34). Some cultures revere the institution for marriage, while in others, the legal, financial, and social ties that held difficult marriages together in the past no longer exist (20). For these and other reasons, it is better to have a clearer understanding of this sacred institution.

I find Kenneth Boa's (7) practical approach to this subject matter most useful in enhancing the basic premise of this book. He believes that marriage is the most significant relationship we can experience. Nevertheless, the institution of marriage has never been more threatened by external and internal problems.

As we shall soon discover, marriage as an institution is challenged from without by a culture which promotes an independent spirit, and minimizes the responsibility of complete commitment. These days, divorce is offered as an increasingly common and acceptable alternative to a committed relationship. Marriage is challenged from within by manipulation, unforgiveness, and a lack of communication

Humankind has virtually ignored the spiritual components of marriage. If we believe and obey God's precepts and principles, our marriages can become increasingly fulfilling and meaningful. Unfortunately, we have not. For that reason, a great deal of pain and suffering continues to plague both marital and family relationships. This underscores the need for this book.

## Purpose of Marriage

A review of the scripture reveals that God instituted marriage. It was divinely designed to be the basic building block of society. In addition, God intended for it to provide an earthly analogy of spiritual truth. Let me repeat that marriage is a lifetime covenant of mutual commitment between a man and a woman, a commitment that leads to oneness on every level: spirit, soul, and body.

This communion and intimacy between marriage partners is designed to reflect the image of God and provide the context for a lasting relationship of love and respect. This relationship, in turn, is the foundation for the privilege of reproduction and the God-given responsibility of physical, psychological, and spiritual nurturing of children (7).

Genesis 1:26-27 states that male and female together constitute the image of God. "And God created man in His own image, in the image of God He created him; male and female He created them" (Gen. 1:27). It is the Lord who created the masculine and the feminine and endowed them with different characteristics so that each expresses something different about God.

We will discover later in this book that these personality differences must be acknowledged and accepted in a healthy marriage. When both partners accept these differences, they become complimentary rather than competitive. The result is synergistic, that is, the total becomes greater than the sum of its parts.

Genesis 1:28-30 describes the divine mandate to the man and the woman: "Be fruitful and multiply, and fill the earth, and subdue it" (vs. 28). God's first command was to reproduce and have dominion over the earth. From the beginning, God made marriage and the family central to His creative and redemptive purposes.

Marriage is a major part of God's plan to bring redemption to the human race. The seed of the marriage relationship provided the vehicle for the incarnation of the savior, Yahshua.

Genesis 2:18-22 reveals that marriage was ordained by God, and not by humankind. It is a covenant relationship, and because it was divinely instituted before the fall (Gen. 3), it was part of God's plan from the beginning. It was not an emergency measure that resulted from sin.

Verse 18 says, "Then the Lord God said, 'It is not good for the man to be alone; I will make him a helper suitable for him.'" God created a sense of need in the man by having him name the animals and so that he would discover that none of them fully corresponded to him. Then from his side God fashioned a new creature that was wonderfully different and yet perfectly complemented the man on a spiritual, intellectual, emotional, and physical level.

Loneliness was replaced by companionship and completion, and this is central to God's design for marriage. The concept of "a helper suitable for him" (vs. 18,20) speaks of a supportive relationship between allies. In no way did it imply that one is inferior to the other.

Genesis 2:23-25 tells us that marriage was designed to be a permanent covenant relationship of mutual commitment, support, and esteem. The man's response in verse 23, "This is now bone of my bones, and flesh of my flesh," is an expression of delight that at last he has found one who corresponds to him. God ordained the marital relationship to be a source of joy and fulfillment, not drudgery.

While Genesis 1-2 portrays the institution of marriage, 1 Corinthians 7 provides specific instructions for marriage. Paul's letter was written to believers in a center of commerce that was noted for moral corruption and sexual promiscuity.

Paul portrays marriage as a reciprocal relationship in which "The wife does not have authority over her own body, but the husband does. Likewise the husband does not have authority over his own body, but the wife does" (vs. 4). Each is enjoined to regularly satisfy the sexual needs of the other ("Let the husband fulfill his duty to his wife, and likewise also the wife to her husband;" vs. 3). In the marital relationship, it is proper for the husband to concern himself with pleasing and serving his wife, and for the wife to desire to please and serve her husband (vs. 33-34).

Genesis 2:24-25 provides the clearest portrait of marriage. It reads:

> For this cause, a man shall leave
> his father and his mother,
> and shall cleave to his wife;
> and they shall become one flesh.
> And the man and his wife were
> both naked and were not ashamed
> (Gen. 2:24-25).

The three elements of leaving, cleaving, and establishing a one-flesh relationship are prerequisites to a healthy marital relationship of commitment, completeness, and companionship.

Leave

Leaving must precede cleaving. Marriage requires the forsaking of other relationships so that the husband and wife can be fully committed to each other. When a man and a woman leave home to start a new family unit, they are no longer under the authority of their parents. They are now directly responsible to God and to each other.

They are to be independent of their parents in a geographical, emotional, and financial sense, and no other relationship should be allowed to come between them. Independence, however, is not the same as avoidance. Scripture requires them to continue to love and honor their parents and to assist them in times of need.

## Cleave

In a relationship of mutual commitment, leaving is the negative aspect, and cleaving is the positive. The marital vows that are expressed in the presence of witnesses establish a permanent covenant in which a man and a woman acknowledge that they are inseparably joined together. The word used in God's mandate for a man to "cleave to his wife" entails the idea of holding fast, of clinging, and of being glued or welded together.

There are many external and internal forces that would threaten to sever this bond. However, a committed couple must remember that both of them have made a solemn vow to cling together through troubled as well as calm waters. As they renew this vow, implement the principles of Scripture, and depend on God's grace, their relationship can continue to grow in spite of trying circumstances.

Although their marriage has priority over everything else including children, friends, career, hobbies, and ministry, cleaving precludes that husband-wife relationship is to be second only to their relationship with the Lord.

## One Flesh

"They shall become one flesh" is the mystery of marriage. While this phrase certainly alludes to the sexual relationship, it goes beyond this, saying that a man and wife actually become one (note that it is a process). The two complete one another physically, psychologically, and spiritually, and this completeness is used in the New Testament to portray an even deeper mystery.

The sexual union was designed by God to be a delightful physical expression of a committed love relationship, and this relationship was in turn designed to portray the spiritual relationship between Yahshua (Jesus) and His bride, the church.

The Scriptures are clear that polygamy, adultery, promiscuity, and divorce distort God's purpose for marriage ( Prov. 5:15-23; 6:32; Mal. 2:16), because such indulgencies minimize its permanency and commitment. Marriage was never intended to be a static or dreary experience that tempts people to look elsewhere for fulfillment. Rather, it is a dynamic process of deepening completeness and companionship. There must be a new identity as two people become one in spirit, soul, and body.

But a growing marriage does not happen by default; it is cultivated by years of mutual effort (discipline) and reliance on the grace of God. When marital problems prevail, they inevitably arise from a failure to leave, cleave, or establish a one-flesh relationship.

## Communication in Marriage

The word communication is derived from the Latin word communis. It simply means to have in common. Commonality is essential to every form of love. Studies consistently reveal that the primary cause of marital problems and divorces is a lack of communication.

Communication is the process of sharing thoughts and feelings, through verbal and non-verbal means with another person so that he or she understands what one is attempting to express to the other. Effective communication does not happen by accident; it is a skill which requires the discipline of development. There are three essential components of the communication process: talking, listening, and caring.

### Talking

The most obvious aspect of communication is verbalizing. Scripture exhorts us to speak the truth in love (Eph. 4:15), and this requires a mutual attitude of openness and honesty. For love to grow in a marriage, there must be regular times of interaction and comradeship. At some point in each day, both partners should make an effort to move beyond the level of routine conversation to verbalize hopes, disappointments, joys, fears, prayer requests and answers, plans, ideas, and interests. As a couple talks things over, confides in each other, and spends time together, they become better and better friends.

One's mate should be his/her best friend. Tragically, this rarely occurs in marriage. Too often, couples get so wrapped up with their children that they hardly know each other. Then when the children leave, they discover that they are like strangers who have been living for years under the same roof, yet feel like total strangers toward each other. This does not need to happen, but effort is required to avoid it.

## Listening

Listening is the biggest problem in effective communication. Most of us have developed poor listening habits. This is especially true in the way we listen to our mates. Because we think we know our partners so well, we often tune them out and miss what they are really trying to say. Preoccupation, daydreaming, worry, distractions (e.g., television), and lack of interest are a few of the barriers to real listening.

Here are several suggestions for improving listening skills:

- Listening requires focused attention. Avoid the temptation of doing other things while conversing with your mate.
- Make an effort to establish good eye contact. Much is communicated through facial expressions and the eyes, so look at your partner, not at the floor, ceiling, or television.
- Because you can think faster than a person can speak, there is a temptation to drift away and get engaged in one's thoughts. Use this extra time by looking for key words, feelings, and subliminal messages. Work on concentrating on what your mate is really saying.
- Show enthusiasm and interest, and be sure to ask probing and clarifying questions to ensure effective communication.
- Try to set aside a special time for undistracted conversation. For many people, the late evening is best.
- Be careful not to interrupt or jump to premature conclusions.
- Look for understanding even when you disagree; try to see issues from your partner's perspective.

Caring

Caring is a key ingredient in effective communication, because it is the genuine desire to understand the other person, to build areas of common ground, and to deepen the relationship. Real caring requires a willingness to concentrate on another person's strengths and accept his or her weaknesses. Caring involves transparency, vulnerability, and supportiveness; it is other-centered rather than self-centered.

Here are some suggestions for developing this aspect of a relationship. Check the areas that need improvement:

- One can enhance positive associations with one's mate by visualizing times of shared joys and experiences and remembering the good things they have done together.
- At least once a year, plan an overnight or a weekend retreat (if you have children, get a baby sitter). Use this time to relax and discuss your marriage, family goals, spiritual life, recreation, finances, and so forth.
- Display physical affection. Touch, pat, hug, and kiss your partner.
- Make it a point to notice and pay attention to your spouse when other people are present.
- Steer away from the habit of nagging and criticism.
- Stretch your sphere of interests to include at least some of your mate's, and look for ways to do things together (gardening, special projects, cultural events, tennis, etc.).
- Compliment your husband or wife whenever possible.
- Don't take your partner for granted; extend the kind of courtesy you showed when you were dating.

Challenges to Marriage

We live in a culture that has succumbed to the process of secularization and one that reflects materialistic values on every level. Though we are supposed to love people and use things, more and more of us use people and love things. Increasing stress and rootlessness, along with confusion of roles and excessive activities, have threatened the stability of the family unit. Communication and creative participation in the home have been on the decline for years. As marital and parental bonds grow weaker, separation and divorce become more common (7). These and other cultural influences challenge the viability of quality marriages as well as affect us all.

The bible is clear in its teaching that marriage is to be permanent ("'For I hate divorce,' says the Lord, the God of Israel;" Mal. 2:16). Separation and divorce are contrary to the purposes for which God instituted marriage. When Yahshua was tested by the Pharisees in this area, He went back to God's original design for marriage, quoting Genesis 1:27 and 2:24 and concluding, "What therefore God has joined together, let no man separate" (Matt. 19:6; Mark 10:9).

When a man and a woman marry, God yokes them in an indissoluble union. It is dishonoring to God to consider divorce as an option because it distorts the spiritual reality of marriage and creates a breach in commitment that can widen under pressure.

We are to pursue a higher standard than that of the prevailing culture. God's pattern and purpose for marriage is constantly imperiled by internal forces of selfishness and by external forces of society. Because of the problem of sin, we all fall short of God's ideal for our marriages. It is only as we abide in His power that we can fulfill His plan in this most important of earthly relationships.

God deals with us in the present (7). If in the past you made mistakes that lead to separation or divorce, you can claim His forgiveness in the present and be relieved from any burden of guilt. Like Paul, you can forget what lies behind and reach forward to what lies ahead (Phil. 3:13).

If in the present you are suffering from an unhappy marriage, you can prayerfully apply biblical principles and maintain your commitment by God's power regardless of the response of your mate. If for the sake of Yahshua you have been called to endure hardship, God's grace will be sufficient for you as you honor Him (Rom. 8:18; 2 Cor. 4:17; 12:9; Phil. 4:13; 1 Pet. 2:19-21; 3:1).

Communion in Marriage

The goal of marriage is communion: a relationship of oneness on the spiritual, psychological, and physical levels.

Spirit

On the deepest level, we are spiritual beings, created in God's image to have an eternal relationship with Him. Nothing short of this relationship will satisfy our God-given needs for unconditional love and acceptance, significance and identity, and competence and achievement.

If we look to our marriage partners to get our personal worth needs met, we will be exploiting the relationship to get something the other person can never deliver. But if we look to Yahshua and daily renew our minds with the truth that our needs are fully met in Him, we will liberate our partners from unrealistic demands and find fulfillment rather than frustration.

When we trust God's love for us and believe His promise that our deepest longings are satisfied in Him, we are then free to give to the other person without expecting or demanding anything in return. Oneness takes place on the spiritual level when both partners look to the Lord to meet their needs and encourage each other to develop this sense of complete dependence. As the two draw nearer to God, they also come closer to each other because both find meaning and fulfillment in the same source.

Triangle of relationships illustration.

Couples can cultivate their spiritual oneness by taking a little time in the morning or evening to study the Bible and pray together. In addition to shared time in prayer and Scripture, it can also be helpful to read and discuss books of mutual interest and listen together to tapes recorded by various Bible teachers.

Soul

On the spiritual level, a husband and wife must depend on the Lord to meet their deepest needs. As they encourage each other to do this, a spiritual oneness develops between them. This in turn is the basis for unity on the psychological level; married couples have been called to an interpersonal oneness of mind, emotion, and will.

While they cannot alter the reality of their security and significance in Yahshua (Jesus), they can enhance each other's realization of this truth. It is natural to desire that our partners reciprocate in this process. However, this desire must not become our goal, since it depends on the other person.

Body

Oneness on the level of spirit and soul provides the basis for physical oneness in marriage. From a biblical standpoint, sex should not be regarded as "making love" but as expressing love. Sexual intimacy was designed to be an expression of spiritual and psychological (mental, emotional, and volitional) intimacy (7). The sexual relationship was never intended to lead to a good marriage, but to be the product of a good marriage.

Our culture has cheapened and debased the idea of sexuality by minimizing this dimension of personal meaning, and ignoring the boundaries originally set by God. Sex has become associated with coarse humor, promiscuity, obsession, perversion, exploitation, and abuse. It is a tyrannical master of those who pursue physical pleasure as a solution for their personal problems.

The biblical perspective is utterly opposed to this mentality. Scripture teaches that God is the originator of the sexual relationship. It is God who designs, but it is man who degenerates.

Believers tend to fall into two basic errors in their attitude toward sex. The first is the Puritanical and Victorian attitude that sex is a kind of necessary evil. This mentality is not derived from the Bible, but from the ancient Greek dualism between the physical (evil) and the spiritual (good).

By contrast, Genesis teaches that marriage and sex were given as a gift of God before, not after the fall. It is therefore good, not sinful, when used according to His design.

While the first basic error deprecates sex, the second error spiritualizes it. It is sometimes described in such elevated terms that one would hardly know that the primary aspect of the sexual relationship is physical and emotional pleasure. Scripture reveals three purposes for the sexual dimension of marriage: procreation, pleasure, and protection (7).

Procreation. The divine mandate to "be fruitful and multiply, and fill the earth" was given before the fall (Gen. 1:28), and after the flood (Gen. 9:7) so that the earth would be populated. Children are the logical outcome of a love relationship.

Pleasure. God created the pleasure of sexuality to enhance this aspect of communication and shared experience (Genesis 3:16; Genesis 18:12; Genesis 26:8; Deuteronomy 24:5;Proverbs 5:18-19), between a man and a wife.

Protection. Another divine purpose for the sexual union between a husband and a wife is to protect them both from immorality:

"But because of immoralities, let each man have his own wife, and let each woman have her own husband. Let the husband fulfill his duty to his wife, and likewise also the wife to her husband. The wife does not have authority over her own body, but the husband does; and likewise also the husband does not have authority over his own body, but the wife does. Stop depriving each other, except by agreement for a time that you may devote yourselves to prayer, and come together again lest Satan tempt you because of your lack of self-control" (1 Cor. 7:2-5).

There are three principal barriers to a fulfilling sexual relationship in marriage. The first arises from painful experiences in the past that relate to sexuality. These can lead to inhibitions and a fear of full participation with one's mate. This obstacle is overcome when a person realizes that his or her needs are fully met in Yahshua, and that rejection or painful associations do not threaten his or her true identity and security.

The second barrier stems from spiritual and/or psychological tension between partners. When there is a lack of caring and communication, when there is anger, guilt, unforgiveness, and resentment, when there is anxiety because of insecurity in the relationship, sexual responsiveness is impaired.

The solution lies in what was said earlier about exchanging goals of manipulation for goals of ministry. When we believe that we are complete in Yahshua (Jesus), we can look beyond ourselves to the needs of our mates and pursue the proper goal of being God's instruments to touch those needs.

The third barrier is poor sexual technique. This can be overcome by a better understanding of the physiological and psychological aspects of romance, warmth, sensitivity, caressing, arousal, etc.

Spiritual, psychological, and physical communion in marriage can continue to grow through the years when a man and a woman are committed to ministering to each other on every level. Physical touching of an affectionate, non-sexual nature (touch should not be used exclusively as a signal for sex) consists of the following:

- Shared feelings
- Closeness without inhibitions
- Absence of psychological defenses
- Open communication and honesty
- Intellectual agreement on major issues
- Spiritual harmony
- Sensitive appreciation of the mate's physical and emotional responses
- Similar values held
- Imparted secrets
- Genuine understanding

- Mutual confidence
- A sense of warmth, safety, and relaxation when together
- Sensuous nearness
- Sexual pleasures lovingly shared
- Signs of love freely given and received
- Mutual responsibility and caring
- Abiding trust

Role of the Husband

Scriptures clearly teach that men and women have distinctive roles to fulfill in marriage, and that these roles actually reflect and illustrate the spiritual relationship between Yahshua and the church.

Ephesians 5:22-33 paints the clearest biblical portrait of the position of the husband and wife. Significantly, this passage is set within the context of the manifestations of the filling of the spirit. Verse 21 tells us that one evidence of the spirit-controlled life is mutual submission in the fear of Yahshua. Submission is not the exclusive responsibility of the woman; it is to be the lifestyle of every believer. One who refuses to live under authority is not fit to wield authority.

Before we can clearly see what the bible means by headship, we need to clear away at least five misconceptions (7):

- Headship is not dictatorship. The Bible does not give the husband permission to set up an autocracy in the home. Husbands are not to lord their authority over their family, but exercise it in humility. Ephesians 5:23 says, "For the husband is the head of the wife, as Yahshua also is the head of the church, He Himself being the Savior of the body." Yahshua is not the dictator but the lover and Savior of the church.
- Headship does not mean that the husband is superior. Men and women have an equal standing before Yahshua (Gal. 3:28). The

best biblical analogy is in 1 Corinthians 11:3--"But I want you to understand that Yahshua is the head of every man, and the man is the head of a woman, and God is the head of Yahshua."

- Headship does not mean that the husband must make all the decisions. Husbands are told to manage their households (1 Tim. 3:12); a wise manager does not make decisions in areas of incompetence, but delegates authority.
- Headship does not mean that the husband is always right. It does mean that he is responsible for the decisions that are made.
- Headship is not to be demanded. Husbands are commanded to love their wives, not to make them submit by lecturing and haranguing them.

The husband's God-given task is nothing less than a leadership of love:

"Husbands, love your wives just as Yahshua loved the church and gave himself for her to sanctify her ... In the same way husbands ought to love their wives as their own bodies." (Eph. 5:25-26,28).

There could be no higher analogy; a husband's love for his wife is to be modeled after Yahshua's supreme passion for the church. This love is rooted in self-sacrifice; like Yahshua, husbands are actually told to give themselves up for the spiritual welfare of their wives. They are called to protect their wives physically, emotionally, and spiritually.

The husband is to be the initiator not only in leadership, but also in love. He is to manifest both authority and affection as head and heart of the home. This provides the perfect balance, because it avoids the two extremes of autocracy (leadership without love) and sentimentality (love without leadership). This can only be achieved by being dependent upon the power of the Holy Spirit.

The Ideal Husband

Ephesians 5:21 introduces the best known passage in Scripture on the role of the husband and wife in marriage. A husband is to be subject to his wife through the proper exercise of his God-given role. Always keep before you this basic relational principle as you proceed through this study.

Leader

The first role of a husband mentioned in Ephesians 5:23 is that he should be the head of the wife.

Head: As God's representative authority, the husband is to take the initiative, leadership, and responsibility for the marriage relationship.

- Being the head means to be the initiator.

Lover

The second role of a husband is that he is to love his wife.

Role of the Wife

The husband is to love his wife as his own body and give himself up for her. The wife is to respect her husband and voluntarily respond to his God-given authority.

Ephesians 5:22-24 and the parallel passage in Colossians 3:18 tell wives to be subject to their own husbands as is fitting in the Lord in the same way that the church is subject to Yahshua.

Many people in our culture have taken issue with this mandate because they misunderstand the New Testament picture of submission. Paul was no woman-hater; his epistles often commend and speak of women with graciousness and respect. It is important to overcome misconceptions in this area:

- Submission does not mean inferiority. In I Peter, there is a clear parallel between Yahshua's submission to "Him who judges righteously" (I Pet. 2:23) and the mandate for wives to be submissive "in the same way" to their own husbands (I Pet. 3:1). This, coupled with the analogy between Yahshua and the Father in I Corinthians 11:3, shows that the wife's role is dignified, not demeaned, because it so clearly reflects the life Yahshua lived.

- Submission does not mean that a wife must place her brain on the shelf. A woman can creatively use her talents and exercise her spiritual gifts within the context of her divinely given role and responsibilities.
- Submission does not mean a lack of fulfillment. True freedom comes from obedience to God's design. Rebellion against biblical truth in an attempt to go one's own way leads to frustration, not fulfillment.

Proverbs 31:10-31 is a beautiful portrait of an excellent wife who has found fulfillment in her God-given role. She recognizes her worth and creatively uses every one of her gifts in the service of her household. Read this passage and list ten of her qualities. How does her husband respond?

- Submission does not mean passivity. It is an active choice that requires the courage of trusting God and depending on Him in the midst of the trials and circumstances of married life.
- Submission does not mean servility. Important decisions in a family should not be made without the perspectives and opinions of the wife. A woman can be outspoken in her ideas and still maintain a biblical attitude toward her husband.

As a wife submits to her husband, she honors God by obeying His design for marriage and reflecting Yahshua's complete submission to His Father:

"In the same way, you wives, be submissive to your own husbands so that even if any of them are disobedient to the word, they may be won without a word by the behavior of their wives, as they observe your chaste and respectful behavior " (I Pet. 3:1-2).

Though Yahshua suffered innocently, He did not lash back. In a similar way, a God-fearing woman is told to be submissive even if her husband fails in his role. Like Yahshua (see I Pet. 2:21-25), she can entrust herself to God, knowing that she is never alone, and believing that the ultimate result of obedience to Him is worth the cost.

The real test is not how others act, but how we react. By God's grace, both men and women should pursue the legitimate goal of being the right person rather than the illegitimate goal of changing their mates' behavior. Because God is loving and good, they can trust Him for the final outcome.

## The Ideal Wife

Ephesians 5:21 introduces the best known passage in Scripture on the role of the husband and wife in marriage. A wife is to be subject to her husband through the proper exercise of her God-given role. Always keep this basic relational principle before you as you proceed through this study.

The primary role of a wife mentioned in Ephesians 5 and I Peter 3 is that she is to be submissive to her husband.

Submission is a voluntary, positive, and respectful response to the God-given authority of the husband.

## Relating to In-Laws

" That is why a man leaves his father and mother . . ." (Gen. 2:24). We have already seen that a successful marriage requires a separation from both sets of parents. This separation can be traumatic to all concerned if the parents have not been preparing their children for the responsibilities of married life. Maturity involves a process of moving from complete dependence to complete independence.

Serious marital problems can develop when this independence is incomplete, especially in the following areas:

(a) Physical. It is not advisable to live with parents or even to spend great amounts of time with them. This can threaten the establishment of a bond of intimacy between a husband and wife.

(b) Emotional. The psychological umbilical cord must be severed, or there will always be the temptation to turn to parents to fulfill roles that should be reserved for your spouse.

(c) Financial. Financial dependence upon parents can lead to domination, low self-esteem, and marital tension.

Another source of strife between couples is an unloving and critical attitude toward in-laws. Even if they are unkind in their treatment, Scripture tells us to respond with kindness, forgiveness, and prayer (see Luke 6:27-28). Paul adds, "Do not be overcome by evil, but overcome evil with good" (Rom. 12:21).

Practical Suggestions

A marriage relationship is never static, but always dynamic. It is either growing or dying. That is why periodic evaluation is always healthy. The following practical suggestions are designed to facilitate the evaluation process. Prayerfully go through the checklist, mark those areas the Holy Spirit impresses upon you, and go to work on them. You'll develop a wonderful marriage in the process!

Suggestions for Husbands

- Find creative ways to do special things for your wife.
- Regularly share your hopes and plans with your wife and listen carefully to hers.
- Be sensitive to her emotional needs and tune in to what she is feeling.
- Look for her strengths and praise her for them.
- Leave her weaknesses to the Lord and pray about them.
- Do not get slack in courtesy and good manners.
- Avoid a domineering and bossy attitude.

- Try to learn new things about her and the things she enjoys.
- Do not compare her with other women.
- Encourage her in her activities.
- Keep yourself spiritually, mentally, and physically fit.

## Suggestions for Wives

- Find creative ways to do special things for your husband.
- Look for his strengths and praise him for them.
- Leave his weaknesses to the Lord and pray about them.
- Try to learn new things about him and the things he enjoys.
- Do not compare him with other men.
- Encourage him in his activities.
- Keep yourself spiritually, mentally, and physically fit.

## Suggestions for Couples

- Study the Bible together and talk about practical applications.
- Pray together on a daily basis.
- Do not criticize, nag, or taunt each other.
- Do your financial planning together. Try hard to reach a unified attitude on credit, spending, and savings. Disharmony over finances is one of the greatest threats to marriage.
- Do not go to sleep with unresolved anger or grievances.
- Practice the art of communication.
- Resolve to make the best of what is rather than fantasizing about what might have been.
- Pursue the goal of ministering to the needs of your mate, knowing that both your needs are already met in Yahshua.
- Notice each other when in public and never make a public remark at the expense of your mate.
- Look for common activities and interests and try to develop them.

- Plan a weekend retreat or vacation alone with your mate at least once a year.

You should now have a clearer understanding of the Divine blueprint for marriage, some problems that could be encountered in your marriage, and how to rise above those challenges. You are now ready to relate to the family unit.

## Definition of Family

The Ashanti tribe in the nation of Ghana, West Africa, has a proverb which says, "The ruin of a nation begins in the homes of its people." I like the essence of that proverb. It would have made my job easier had the Ashanti proverb provided a definition for 'family'. Obviously, this proverb assumed the meaning of 'family' was understood.

Let me wrestle with that definition for now. The term 'family' means different things to different people. An economist might perceive a family as two or more persons related by blood, marriage, or adoption, and residing together.

To a sociologist, a family is a primary social group in any society, typically consisting of a man and a woman, or any two individuals who wish to share their lives together in a long-term commitment to each other, bring up offspring and usually reside in the same dwelling.

It might also mean a primary social group; parents and children; people descended from a common ancestor; a collection of things sharing a common attribute

To a biologist, the same term means a taxonomic group containing one or more genera. To complicate matters, different cultures that believe in the extended family system might have different definitions for a family.

Consider the following definition cited by Hopkinson (21). It conveys the gist of what I have in mind when I use the term family in this book:

I am aware that some people can boast of a successful marriage. Others might rate their marriage as fair.

Nevertheless, one problem or another characterizes the majority of marriages all over the world. In other words, there is no perfect marriage.

If your marriage is good, I believe you can use some advice to make it better. If it is on the rocks, believe me, you can rise above the challenges you face; if it is somewhere in the middle, I trust that you would at least hold your ground or move up several notches with the invaluable information presented in this book.

I urge you to wake up and realize that you cannot allow yourself to hope against hope. There is no situation you are facing now that is completely new on earth. Others have gone through similar or worse situations, and some have come through such situations. So can you. I hope I have steered your thinking in the right direction regarding the marriage and family institutions.

You can do it. You owe it to yourself, and your family. I am here to help you try to overcome the issues in your marriage or relationship. If no one else cares, remember I do, and that is why I have written this book. If no one else seems to understand, I do. E-mail me because I am on your side.

Let us now get on the road to certain key pre-marital elements that must be firmly, and systematically understood and implemented in order to establish a solid basis for a successful, rewarding marriage and family relationship.

Marriage is the expression of heterosexual identity (13). Therefore, it is important to understand gender relations as they pertain to this sacred institution. I have taken the liberty to transpose the foregoing concepts and principles of Divine blueprint for marriage in a more circular format for the benefit of those who prefer that approach. This has been done following a model on gender relation proposed by Dr. Leon James of the University of Hawaii (22). He gives the reader the opportunity to examine gender behavior in the context of marriage by identifying the sub-components of gender habits in men and women. The three domains of behavior are: sensorimotor, cognitive, and affective.

The basic premise of this model is that it is the idea that a man and a woman can form a special and unique relationship in marriage. They can become unified at all three levels of the "threefold self" (22)--in sensory-motor behavior, in thinking operations, and in feeling states. But there are barriers or resistances to overcome with each level of the unification or conjoining process.

The first level of unity is sensorimotor. This involves what the couple does together externally or socially. The second level is cognitive, involving how each person thinks and whether he or she agrees in definitions and beliefs. The third and deepest level is affective. This involves what the person feels and what motivates him/her to achieve

## The Individual's Threefold Self

Gender behavior in marriage is defined along three interacting domains called the individual's threefold self. The individual's affective self operates the feelings and motivations we maintain in dating or marriage relationships. The cognitive self operates the thinking and reasoning we process in these relationships. The individual's sensorimotor self operates the sensations, perceptions, and motor acts performed in gender relationships.

The category of "motor acts" includes overt verbal behavior (discourse, talk) and non-linguistic behaviors (expressions, appearance, and style). Be aware, however, that motor acts and talking occur not from themselves, but from cognitive acts (our thinking and lifestyle philosophy).

These in turn occur from our affective acts, which are motivations and needs that guide our thinking toward goals. Sensorimotor acts, cognitive acts, and affective acts form a perfect synergy among feelings, thoughts, and actions. This is called the threefold self.

Affective operations guide and influence the direction of operations in the cognitive self, so that what we think or how we justify things cognitively is selective and responsive to our affective motives. We entertain a way of thinking that will support and promote our motivations and feelings. Our cognitive behavior adjusts itself to support our affective behavior.

The affective and the cognitive domains together select and determine the overt sensorimotor behavior of our overt actions, appearance, words, and styles. What we do and say (overt gender behavior) is the result of what we think, which is the result of how we feel (what motivates us). Note that we are often more aware of what we think than of how we feel (or what motivates us).

In relationships between a man and a woman, the woman tends to be more aware of her own feelings and motivations than the man is aware of his own feelings and motivations. Generally, this is because women are more motivated to spend time and focus figuring out how they really feel or what they really want.

A woman tends to be more in tune with a man's feelings and motivations than a man is of his own feelings and motivations. However, this does not mean that men have fewer feelings than women, as is sometimes misrepresented in gender-stereotyped thinking.

Both men and women have equal amounts of feelings and emotions. When observed and analyzed, they react to things moment by moment--with surprise, or with anger, or being pleased or displeased, feeling like talking or feeling like keeping quiet, being in a good mood or bad, getting excited when telling a story, picking a fight, feeling resentful, liking something, appreciating something, feeling happy about something, etc. These observations prove that men equally with women have feelings and react with emotions all the time.

Feelings and emotional reactions are a necessary part of all thinking and acting (22). It is not possible to act and react in a conversation or interaction without feelings and motivations being present. In gender relations, women are motivated more than men in focusing consciously on feelings.

This difference in the skill of gender perceptiveness between a man and a woman creates an active gender dynamic in which the woman is motivated to prod her man to become more aware of his and her feelings and motivations. The man tends to resist this "affective prodding" and finds it unpleasant and objectionable. This creates a constant strain on the developing relationship. The woman feels that the man doesn't want to "commit" and is resisting the process of conjunction, thereby maintaining in them a state of division and conflict which is not totally satisfying to the woman.

Both men and women can gain understanding of the initial oppositeness between the sexes--women striving to conjoin, men resisting the process. The analysis of how men and women speak with each other reveals this dynamic opposition between the sexes. Analyzing verbal interactions between men and women is a powerful method for bringing out differences. They use conversation to oppose each other or to gain deeper intimacy and mutual support.

The individual's threefold self in gender relationships is a joint product of biological, sociological, cultural and spiritual make up (22). As children, we acquire the relationship style of our parents, other adults, and the media (TV, movies, songs, magazines, cartoons, commercials). By the time we begin adolescent or adult relationships, we have been exposed to years of stereotyped gender behaviors in all three domains of the threefold self:

- Exploitative feelings towards the opposite sex (affective self),
- Sexist thoughts that stereotype the other gender (cognitive self),
- Injurious or hostile actions and words against the partner (sensorimotor self).

When couples have a disagreement, physical and mental abuse is practiced more often by men than women.

When people reason under the influence of exploitative motivations, they tend to misinterpret the intentions of their partner. They tend to use stereotyped, inaccurate, and prejudiced thinking. Our verbal behavior will reflect this style of biased thinking. So will our other actions.

There is an advantage in gaining control over our gender behavior in the three domains-- sensorimotor, cognitive, and affective. We can avoid those cultural, psychological traits and habits that interfere with adaptive, successful marriage relationships. The benefits of a stable successful long term partnership are attractive. We will explore a particular principle in marriage relationship called 'conjoint self.'

Dr. James contends that the perfection of unity in a marriage increases through differentiation and reciprocity of behavior in the threefold self of the two partners, and it is a spiritual union that last to eternity. In a unity marriage, the husband and wife develop a conjoint self, while their former individual self recedes into the background.

He believes marriage is not achieved by promise or desire alone. There are developmental levels of unity that married partners must go through. The growth process takes many years of dedicated effort. The "conjoint self" refers to a husband or a wife who has achieved unity at all levels of the threefold self (as explained in the following).

Each individual has been changed, with some traits eliminated and new ones that fit together acquired. This is called growing together in reciprocity. The husband must abandon some traits he cherished since childhood because these habits cause opposition and disunity. The wife must abandon traits that she perceives do not fit with her husband's character.

Both must acquire new traits that fit together as a unit. The old traits that have been abandoned and the new traits that have been acquired consist of sensorimotor, cognitive, and affective traits in the threefold self. That is, habits of external activities, habits of thinking, and habits of internal feeling.

Levels of unity are ordered from external to more interior unity, as will be explained below. An external level of unity between marital partners involves their sensorimotor portion of the threefold self. They like and enjoy doing things together like dancing, touching each other, partying, camping, watching movies, eating out, driving, talking about their favorite topics, and so on.

These overt "external" activities involve sensory and motor interactions, including verbal, which is an overt motor activity. Every sensorimotor activity involves thinking and feeling but these cognitive and affective operations are not visible. The focus of

the two partners at this stage is each other's external activity. There is less focus or concern on what the other is thinking or feeling.

Note that these joint external activities do not necessarily mean the two partners are in agreement with each other's way of thinking, attitudes, feelings or motivations. The cognitive and affective self of each partner may not be in agreement. One may even be competitive or hostile to the other. The inside that is not visible (affective and cognitive self) may be in opposition and experiencing hatred toward the partner, while the exterior--the sensory-motor activity, may appear harmonious and compatible.

Disagreement or dislike becomes visible when there is an overt fight during which the two partners show their anger, resentment, and disrespect toward each other. Afterwards, as they make up, the cognitive disrespect and affective dislike recede into the underlying invisible state, until the next fight ensues again, at which time the abuse and disrespect arise.

There is a *first level* of the conjoint self. This external level, involving sensorimotor reciprocity and joint achievement, exists without there necessarily being an interior agreement and respect for the partner. Women, more than men, tend to experience this external phase of the relationship as unsatisfactory, painful, and injurious. Women often bond with other women for support and reassurance during this phase of disharmony.

Men tend to bond with other men by complaining about women and speaking about them with disrespect. Men keep secrets from their women and do things they want to hide from them. Men do this in order to obtain sexual favors. This deception is a method of exploiting women and dehumanizing them. At this external level of unity, men feel more comfortable than women because they exercise control in the relationship.

Men tend to resist closer, more intimate relationship phases in order to maintain their cognitive and affective independence. A man dislikes giving up independence in his private thinking and feeling, while a woman is generally motivated to conjoin her thinking and feeling with her man--if only he lets her. A woman strives to achieve mutual and reciprocal dependence, while a man strives to retain independence. This creates a conflict dynamic between them, especially in the first level of unity, which is external, involving the sensorimotor self only.

This intrinsic difference between women and men occurs at all levels of their humanity: biological, mental, and spiritual. Biologically, women make themselves dependent on men for reproduction, parenting, and lifestyle habits. Mentally, women love and enjoy the man's intelligence and inventiveness, adopting his ideas and philosophies. Spiritually, women represent inner wisdom surrounded by external love. Men represent inner love surrounded by external intelligence. Women and men are born reciprocals of each other. They may better fit into a perfect unity.

If women and men were similar in these fundamental traits, they could only form external relationships and could never achieve the married state of the conjoint self. Their individual selves would remain separate because like cannot conjoin with like. Like can be adjoined to like, but only reciprocals can conjoin. Think of the shape of reciprocals and how they would not be able to fit together if they were similar instead of reciprocal: pot and handle; key and key hole; shoe and lace; button and button hole, snaps, window and window sill, picture and frame, etc.

Couples begin their relationship together by sensorimotor reciprocity talking to each other, eating, dancing, driving, and doing fun things. This is the first level of unity.

The second level of unity is deeper in that it involves the cognitive self of the two partners. This includes how they think, how they reason, how they justify things, what they consider acceptable or unacceptable, what information or knowledge they have, and their philosophy of life and religion. These cognitive behaviors and habits are resistant to mutual adaptation and reciprocity in the relationship. A man and a woman may be married for years and yet maintain contradictory attitudes, beliefs, and judgments.

The external sensorimotor level of unity does not necessarily lead to a more interior unity of thinking and reasoning (cognitive habits). Yet many couples achieve a cognitive level unity by joint involvement in running a home and raising children. They see 'eye to eye' on many things and enrich each other's thinking process by mutual

stimulation and interest. When a man and a woman achieve this second level unity, they love each other more deeply. The relationship continues to grow and becomes more satisfying and enriching.

Achieving cognitive reciprocity is easier for women because they are mentally oriented towards conjunction. They desire to become a conjoint self more than they desire to retain their own ideas and philosophy. Men generally are in love with their own thinking and ideas and resist change for the sake of the conjoint self. Men see the conjoint self as giving up selfhood, while women see it as gaining togetherness.

However, when a wife perceives that her husband's thinking is corrupt, she attempts to alter the man's thinking instead of adopting it for herself. A wife has a keen perception of what her husband's corrupt thinking is, even while he, himself, is blind. This is because spiritually, "a woman is inner wisdom covered with love, while a man is inner love covered with external intelligence."

So a woman perceives more with her inner wisdom, while a man with his outward intelligence. Inner wisdom can see corrupted thinking where outward intelligence cannot. Outward intelligence is motivated by sensorimotor goals, while inner wisdom is motivated by affective goals. But when the husband allows his outward intelligence to be influenced by the wife's inner wisdom, his outward intelligence is elevated or made more efficient. He, too, can perceive corrupt thinking in himself and others.

The innermost level of unity involves the partners' affective self -- their feelings, motivations, love, ultimate goals of happiness and togetherness. Affective reciprocity is the basis of an eternal unity between husband and wife. Only conjoint feelings, love, desires, or goals are allowed to remain operational in their mind. This is achieved by a systematic and long-term effort in reciprocal growth.

A partner abandons his/her feelings, loyalties, goals, or involvements that are not conjoint and exclude the other. Affective reciprocity or conjunction would be weakened if one partner reserves an area of his/her mind or involvement that excludes the other partner. For example, some husbands spend socializing time with male friends. The activity is such that they don't want wives or girl friends around, even if they are not cheating on them or not hiding anything.

But the fact that a husband's wife is excluded, not wanted there, means that he is retaining independent involvements and loves. These affective habits and enjoyments are not reciprocal. They do not contribute to unity in marriage, but slows the process down or acts against it.

However, this principle does not apply to women in the same way. Women have loyalties and friendships among themselves for different goals and feelings than men have with each other. The affections and involvements that married women have with other women are for supporting the marriage, not resisting it.

Men have an inborn resistance to marital unity which they have to fight against most of their life (22). Their male friendships that exclude the wife respond to their desire to escape total unity with their wife. This is not so with married women since they have an inborn desire and need for total unity with their husband.

Many organizations have instituted family life and marriage education among their membership. This is an important step in the right direction. However, since all of our actions usually originate in our minds, an understanding of the reasons why people choose to get married will be necessary in order to ascertain whether or not our decisions are in God's plan.

# CHAPTER 4

## Does Your Decision to Marry Fit into the Divine Plan?

### My Personal Testimony

My parents had been married for a little over 60 years. It is generally thought that couples who grew up in stable homes tend to have more successful marriages. As such, I often wondered why the many battles I had with my previous relationships.

I felt comfortable talking to my mother about the facts of life. My dad was a great father. However, he was an introvert. He often maintained an even demeanor, and rarely showed his emotions.

He was a hard-core Presbyterian, overly cautious not to make mistakes, and was there for his children mostly for material support. He read widely, and was a tacit politician. He never gave straight answers to questions. Rather, he preferred to provide a number of scenarios and expected you to pick the most appropriate path for your situation. I did not appreciate that technique at that time. However, I do now understand his rationale.

During a candid conversation concerning my love life with my mother several years ago, she told me that I would "know" when the right person came along. She added a few other points to her advice. I have found these not only invaluable but duplicated in the literature.

She advised me to ascertain a prospective mate's readiness to invest in a committed relationship. In addition; my mother encouraged me to evaluate her ability to communicate openly, and effectively. Finally, she cautioned me to ascertain the importance we attached to each other in the relationship.

Communication in that case meant how well my prospective mate and I understood each other's point of view. It is important to know whom to trust with such matters.

Why? Because some of the people you might think would understand and sympathize with your demise might not necessarily have your best interests at heart.

I knew my mother would always tell me the truth, even if it hurts, and steer me in the right direction. Little did I know I would have the opportunity to experience her advice only a few years later.

I have held several management positions in my career. During my tenure as Corporate Business Development Manager for an engineering consulting firm in Houston, I had the opportunity to attend a meeting, together with counterparts from other similar companies.

The meeting was originally scheduled with the then mayor of the City of Houston. Unfortunately, he could not make it to that meeting due to some newsworthy event that required his presence at another place. He, therefore, asked the City Administrator to sit in for him.

After being in that position for few months, I learned rather quickly that a little aggressiveness, coupled with a carefully crafted tacit message could do wonders for a marketing person. Sometimes only a few seconds or minutes might make the difference between getting your point across to a target potential client. I took advantage of that opportunity to chat with the City Administrator. I asked for his guidance in helping me broaden my contacts at the city.

In following up a number of leads provided by the City Administrator, I had the opportunity to meet a nice young lady who worked for the City of Houston. She was a Division Manager with the Public Works Department. She later introduced me to the Director of that Department. The first time I went to her office, I was accompanied by one of my colleagues. When she came down the hallway to meet us, I felt something significantly different about her. I was wise enough to know not to mix business with pleasure.

Therefore, I immediately concealed my observations and feelings. Unfortunately, my colleague also noticed what he later termed 'good chemistry' between me and that lady. I pretended I did not hear what he said.

On the way to pick up my car and return to the office, my colleague and I noticed our car was towed because of an expired time on the parking meter. Guess whom we called to give us a ride to get our car from the storage place? It was the director of public works with whom we just met.

He asked his division manager to give us a ride to the storage facility where our car was towed. We got our vehicle back. Strangely, on our way back to the office, I heard the song, "Why Do Fools Fall in Love." come on the car radio.

I interpreted that as an omen. I also thought about the lyrics of Kenny Rogers's song cautioning the listener not to 'Fall in Love with a Dreamer, because when you think you've really changed him, he'll leave you again.'

Over the years, I have come to expect resistance to come my way whenever I engaged in something good. The enemy is a spirit. It sees ahead of time when something good is coming your way, or if you are engaged in something good. Subsequently, It would attempt to thwart it.

However, I heard the resonating words of my mother ringing in my ears over and over again. It was as if designed to counteract those doubtful thoughts. Therefore, I knew something good was about to happen to me. I was determined not to allow the enemy or the spirit of doubt or fear to prevail upon me.

Remember our basic premise that most of the root causes of our problems are Spiritual? By the time you finish reading this book, you will know how to listen and follow your inner teacher at crucial times like that.

To cut a long story short, a permanent relationship developed between the division manager and me. I am talking about my wife, Denise. I finally found her. I knew it when I did. No one had to tell me. My mother was right after all.

However, my mother is not around to celebrate that good news with me. I know she is watching us from a better place, and enjoying every bit of the happiness I now share with Denise. That was my lot. Yours might come in a different way. For now, allow me to share with you some reasons why people get married to a particular person.

I would like to put you on the road to a happier marital life. Allow me to help you make this transition in a systematic way. Here is how it begins.

## Food for Thought

The concept of the blending of two lives into one is much easier said than done. There are bound to be difficulties and, believe me, differences do arise. Take a look around you. There are numerous books and seminars on marriage. People buy these books and attend such seminars in hopes of finding some secret formula for a happy and peaceful relationship. They desire to know the secret that would hopefully allow them to live together happily ever after.

After the wedding ceremony, a married couple basks in the excitement, glamour and thrill of having found true love and happiness. As they breathe the air of importance and accomplishment, they tend to overlook the potential lurking of danger that sometimes surfaces unexpectedly. One such danger could be that you may not know the person you got married to as well as you thought.

The danger I am referring to knows no bounds. It may even rear its ugly head in the family of respected members of the clergy. For example, recently in Tennessee the wife of a beloved pastor allegedly shot and killed her husband. Subsequently, she drove off with their three daughters to the State of Alabama.

One only needs to turn on the television set to listen to other horrible stories like the elusive Nicole Simpson case, or that of Scott Peterson, or Terry Shiavo. Was anyone able to predict the outcomes of such marriages?

How often do we hear of many teenage girls or sometimes boys assaulted or molested by their parents or step-parents? Some authorities believe there could be as high as 50% of incestuous relations in American homes. Only a small percentage of such horrible activities are reported.

Men and women differ both physically and emotionally. First year biology books teach some of these basic differences. For example, men are generally stronger, and bigger, while women tend to be relatively smaller. As previously discussed in Chapter 2 of this book, emotional differences also exist. Women tend to have a higher emotional sensitivity than men, and their emotional pendulum swings widely from great highs to lows, compared to men's.

Against these as well as other basic differences, God established rules of relationship between husband and wife. These rules must be followed in order to find fulfillment, joy, and happiness. However, if these rules are ignored serious problems set in. Unfortunately, people don't always agree in practice with God's rules. Dating back to African, Greco-Roman, Asiatic and Jewish philosophies, the husband was the recognized head of household.

Western Christian ethic, on the other hand, uniquely establishes a reciprocal relationship. These are depicted in the Book of Ephesians in the New Testament. It spells out the wife's obligation to the husband, and vice versa. Furthermore, it defines the child's obligation to the parent, and the parent's obligation to the child.

Let me say that Western Christian ethics do not connote submission of ungodly demands of husbands. In that chain-of-command, God is head over the husband. If the husband is not a Godly man, then the wife should be in submission to God, first. In other words, she must skip over the broken link. For this reason, it is very important for a woman to choose wisely the man she marries. Better yet, in order to avoid such difficulties, the Bible encourages believers 'not to be unequally yoked.' Yet people sometimes ignore such admonition and get married to a prospective mate, anyway.

## Major Reasons Why People Get Married

There are many reasons why people decide to get married (42). It would be impossible to list them all in this book. However, the major reasons include:

- Need to be loved
- Financial security
- Companionship/Overcoming loneliness
- Sexual fulfillment
- Solution to personal problems
- Avoid living in 'sin,' and
- Raising a family

After interviewing several 'happily married couples,' divorce attorneys, religious leaders, and reviewing several hundred pages of literature on marriage, I came to the conclusion that no one other than God has the correct formula for a successful marriage, as described in Chapter I of this book. My understanding of the Divine Blueprint for marriage together with supporting references in the scriptures lead me to believe that one must look before leaping into a marriage. How does one accomplish that, you might ask?

### Look before you leap

Marriage is serious business. It requires very careful thought, planning, evaluations, and investigations before one makes a final decision to 'tie the knot.' By all means, do not jump into a permanent relationship just for selfish gains.

One might ask, "How do I look?" To answer that, let us go back to our basic premise in the first Chapter of this book, "Render unto Caesar the things that are Caesar's and unto God the things that are God's." What this means is, that one must use all of the tools God endowed him or her with in the observation, evaluation, selection, and proposition phase to God. Secondly, and most important of all, one must submit the 'proposal' to God for His approval.

Two Bible passages come to mind immediately, "Man proposes but God disposes", and "Trust in the Lord with all your heart, and lean not unto your own understanding. In all your ways, acknowledge Him, and He will direct thy paths." A path not ordered by God is one that causes one to enter the Kingdom by the Broad Gate. One directed by God, lead to the 'Narrow Gate' of true love, life, happiness, success, and prosperity!

The beginning of the answer to the question posed in the preceding paragraph is to use all of our seven points of communication with God. These are: sight, smell, taste, hearing, taste, solar plexus, and our intuition. This is just the start. In addition, look for signs of body language during early dating (6,11,19). Here are some pointers for your consideration:

- A person full of smiles is most likely an open, positive person.
- Nodding, and vocal signals. Nodding could indicate affirmation or agreement. On the contrary, frequent pauses, or short answers where expected could indicate a lack of interest or concealment of information.
- Leaning appropriately toward the opposite sex could signify an interest or desire to engage with the person of interest.
- An appropriate touch might be interpreted as a point of contact or expression of caring. I am assuming that the reader is conversant with 'Sexual Harassment Laws,' where applicable. Similarly, a person's posture could be a reflection of his/her level of self-confidence.
- Be observant on your date, and maintain proper eye contact. This indicates respect, trust, caring, sincerity, or attention. People usually like it when their dates make them feel very special. In this regard, ensure that you look at the person directly. Remember, if the person focuses on your lips while you are talking, that could be an indication of what they could have on their mind. They might be imaging what it would feel like to kiss you!
- In a calculated manner, mirror the positive behavior of the person of interest. People tend to like others who have similar behavioral patters as they do. Remember, crossed arms, closed hands, holding arms across the chest, clasping hands, or crossing legs away from the other person are considered closed positions, and may not be mirrored.
- Point your body in their direction.

After the initial screening process outlined above, it might be wise for you to consider the following preliminary elements (35) provided below, as you continue to develop your relationship with the person of interest:

- Be yourself. More often than not people who are considering marriage go through great lengths and expense to 'package' themselves in images they are not. They change their hairstyles, clothing, and lose weight, find new lines of makeup, and use other paraphernalia to make them strikingly attractive. Eventually, after the marriage, the screen that camouflaged their natural selves come unveiled. This smokescreen can lead to disastrous consequences. Be the best that you be, and let your prospective partner accept you for who you really are.

- Have a clear profile of whom you really want. Do not settle for less than that. Many people make terrible mistakes by thinking that because the ratio of women to men is tilted in favor of women the competition for the few 'available good men' is too keen to pick and choose whom one really wants. They settle for less than what they could have had. It is a fact that more baby girls than boys are born on earth. I will encourage you to believe that God has a master plan for your life, and has prepared someone especially for you.

- Be able to distinguish between 'dreamers' and real people. There are lots of fake people out there. They would do almost anything to win your love under the guise of 'compatibility.' That is not to say that everybody out there is a fake. There are a bunch of liars and great pretenders, and 'show boaters' out there. With the advent of recent technology, people find ways and means to obtain personality profiles, inheritance information, credit reports, income, and all sorts of information on people they could use to their advantage.

- Take initiative to look for a life-long partner. I call that 'Faith in Action.' Oh Yes! I believe in the power of God to provide all of our needs exceeding abundantly above and beyond what we imagine. Faith and receptivity are crucial in this regard. We must put a little faith in action and count on Him to guide us. Do not be afraid to seek help and advice from trusted friends, if possible. Seek advice from people who know you or your potential partner well.

- Use all the points of communication with God to determine compatibility with your potential mate. Do not be misled by 'love at first sight.' Some people operate under the premise that what they see is what they would end up with. Distinguish between inward and outward beauty, outward and inward attraction. Life is a one way street that leads to a permanent destination. The mystery of it is that no one returns to tell you what really goes on at the end of that final destination. Too many things happen in life to base a life-long relationship upon a single factor such as good sex, which many people erroneously fail to realize. What happens, for example, if your mate is placed on certain high blood pressure medication, which is very effective in controlling his blood pressure, but makes him temporarily impotent? What would you do if you were attracted to your mate because her hair color and length, and then later in life she develops breast cancer, and is placed on chemotherapeutic drugs which cause her hair to fall out?

- Learn to place yourself under Divine order. He will guide your decisions and actions. Do your best to solve or resolve any issues in your life before you make the final decision to get married. Do not presume your potential mate holds all the right keys to get you out of misery. Or that you would get what you want if you give them what they want. That could be a terrible mistake.

- Know your strengths and weaknesses, especially how they complement one another. Examine yourself and make appropriate changes genuinely. King David overestimated his strength in resisting the powers of a woman. He looked at a woman bathing for too long, and ended up a murderer and an adulterer. On the other hand, Joseph did not underestimate the power of an adulterous woman. He took no chances with Portifar's wife. Ultimately, he became Prime Minister of Egypt. I know a very attractive lady who was raised in a good home. She is well behaved, cooks well, holds great conversations, and is very well educated. However, she has difficulties keeping relationships because she has a quick temper, and tends to be domineering.

- Ensure you are both committed and proud of each other in the relationship.

- Do not be 'unequally yoked.' Take one day at a time, and treat each day as special.

- Get to know your partner well enough to determine the expectations of the union you are about to make.

- What would you expect could be different later on in the marriage?

- Agree on where you plan to establish residence.

- Decide on apportionment of financial responsibility.

- Settle on the issue of having or not having children, how many, and the responsibilities that go along with raising children or step-children (30).

- How forgiving (29) is either of you, and how well do you work out your differences? Can you really go to bed each night without being angry at each other?

- Can both of you make a conscious effort to agree to make the relationship work no matter what?

- How much fun do you have with each other? How well do you understand and cope with each other's moods or feelings? Becoming friends before lovers certainly applies well in this instance.

I hope you have gotten the idea by now that the decision to marry involves a lot of thought and work. Arranged marriages, with input from parents and or other more 'experienced' relatives, do not always work. You need the power of God on your side to make the final decision.

Marriage is like building a good house. If a lot is invested into preparing the right foundation, then the structure built on the foundation will remain on solid rock, and not on shifting sand. When the storms come against it, such a structure will stand, and not fall. Ninety percent of your happiness or misery could ride on laying the right foundation for your marriage. Do not take it lightly. You must have God's direction on your side.

The need to establish and enjoy a healthy marital and family relationship is long overdue. Yet, it is an investment that pays off well for all. Make it your business to promote it anyway you can, even if that means supporting political candidates who are cognizant of that fact. Simply stated, the socio-economic impacts of marital breakdown are too costly to be ignored. Let us take a closer look at this factor in the next chapter.

# CHAPTER 5

## The Prohibitive Cost of Marital and Family Breakdown

The overwhelming reason for writing this book is to save marriage and strengthen family relationships. No one holds the 'Magic Wand' to guarantee a successful and happy marriage. There are many books, seminars, and counselors who do their best to alleviate or save perilous marriages and relationships. The fact that marriage relationship breakdowns are still rampant globally leads me to believe that additional work needs to be done.

I have come to discover that most of the issues of relationship and family breakdown are spiritual rather than physical. As such, we must couple the current strategies with spiritual elements if we are to succeed. That is to say, we must go back to the Creator who formulated the marriage institution for answers, and expects strong family relationships in His creation.
If you get Him on your side, He will guide you through the numerous perils in life, including your marriage and relationship issues.

God does not like divorce. If we know the root causes of divorce, we should be able to salvage most relationship breakdowns in order to please Him and ourselves.

There are several factors that contribute significantly to marriage and relationship breakdown. These factors fall within socio-economic, cultural, and inter-personal realms. In the subsequent chapter, I will discuss what physiological and spiritual elements are that could also militate against marriage and family relationship.

One might ask, " Are we only interested in saving marriages just to please God and ourselves?" The resounding answer is, "No." Marriage breakdown exacts a substantial cost on every nation. The cost is both direct and indirect. Let us look at cost breakdowns examples from selected developed nations. This is necessary if we are to rely on accurate information.

## Direct costs

Despite the overwhelming evidence of the benefits of marriage to families and society, the sad fact remains that, for more than four decades, the welfare system has penalized and discouraged marriage. The U.S. welfare system is currently composed of more than 70 means-tested aid programs providing cash, food, housing, medical care, and social services to low-income population. Each year, over $200 billion flows through this system to families with children (25).

In recognition of the widespread benefits of marriage to individuals and society, the federal welfare reform legislation enacted in 1996 set forth clear goals: to increase the number of two-parent families and to reduce out-of-wedlock childbearing. Regrettably, in the years since this reform, most states have done very little to advance these objectives directly. Out of more than $100 billion in federal Temporary Assistance to Needy families (TANF) funds disbursed over the past seven years, only about $20 million--a miniscule 0.02 percent--has been spent on promoting marriage.

These programs have also been shown to be effective in reducing domestic violence. The pro-marriage initiative would not merely seek to increase marriage rates among target couples, but also would provide ongoing support to help at-risk couples maintain healthy marriages over time.

For the sake of comparison, let us look at available statistics in the country of Australia. Marriage and relationship breakdown is a direct cost to the Commonwealth budget in the form of social security payments, family court costs, legal aid, the child support scheme, and taxation rebates, as the following calculations indicate:

> "the Department of Social Security spent a little over $3 million on the Sole Parent Pension, the Child Support Scheme and Jobs Education and Training (JET) in 1996-97."

About 70 per cent of Sole Parent Pensioners were people who had been married or de facto married but had separated or divorced. Approximately $2,200 million of the expenditure is referable to marriage and relationship breakdown:

- the Family Court of Australia costs $112 million to operate in 1996-97.

- Legal Aid spent approximately $40 million on Family Court cases in 1994-95.

- the Child Support Scheme cost $169 million to run in 1996-97.

- the Sole Parent Tax Rebate cost Commonwealth revenue $250 million in 1994-95.

These items total $2,771 million annually. The figure is necessarily conservative. Other costs could be rightfully included in the cost of marriage and relationship breakdown, but it is difficult to separate the components. For example, expenditure on emergency accommodation and the homeless allowance partly arises from marriage breakdown, but it has not been possible to determine the size of this part.

The above information clearly shows the exorbitant direct costs to the United States and Australia, as a result of marriage breakdown. Nevertheless, these are only two countries. If the total direct cost could be computed for half of the nations of the world, the impact would be very dramatic.

That is not the entire story, however. There are indirect costs that must be reckoned with. Again, in the interest of time and availability of accurate records, I would again like to focus on the above two countries for this factor.

Indirect cost
A review of the literature indicates that poor health is partially a consequence of marriage and relationship breakdown. The extent of this cost to the nation is immeasurable. It extends not only to physical and mental health, but also to the social pathologies such as child and family abuse. Similarly, absenteeism in the work force

and low productivity have been linked to relationship problems. Professor John Gottman estimates that for the US, approximately 30 per cent of sick time is due to family conflict.

Marriage and family breakdown costs the Australian nation at least $3 billion each year. When all the indirect costs are included, the figure is possibly double. When the personal and emotional trauma involved is added to these figures, the cost to the nation is enormous.

In comparison, the Commonwealth government spends just $3.5 million annually on preventive marriage and relationship education programs, and $2.05 million on parenting skills training. This is a 1000 fold difference. The imbalance is manifest. It requires correction. (25)

In light of the foregoing, it seems plausible that every effort must be made to promote healthy marriages throughout the world. Many nations believe in the separation of church and state. However, I have come to discover that proper leadership of a nation entails mutual cooperation between these two entities.

In this regard, it might be proper to incorporate or enhance various tools available to predict the possible outcome of a pending or proposed marriage before actual execution of the union takes place. At this juncture, I would like to present certain pointers for the reader's consideration.

Let me say that this chapter presented me with one of the most difficult dilemmas in writing this book because it was very difficult to pin point just one, two, or three factors that cause breakdowns in relationships. That means the causes of marital and relationship breakdowns are not only complex and diverse; they are in most cases interactive.

To compound the problem, it was evident that the views for marital and relationship breakdowns varied depending on the background and social status of the various individuals in view.

To further compound the problem, the cost of marital and/or family breakdown cannot only be measured in monetary values. It can be very costly in human terms. Let us examine some negative impacts of divorce and relationship breakdown on children.

### Children

Remember that the focal point of this book is to save marriages and strengthen family relationships. The general consensus among most people is that marriage, at its height, should result in procreation of children. However, as we have previously noted, the fruit of the womb is a gift from God. In His Divine Wisdom, He chooses to give that good gift to some but not to others. I do not know why that is so. But I have come to discover that God will always make the best decisions in our own best interests.

We are human and can only see so far. God is God. He can see way into the future. Think of it like this. Assume you had a connection to a flawless satellite in space. This satellite can see far ahead of you. It can provide details about your path, obstructions on your path, enemy positions and movement, type of equipment and vehicles the enemy has in his or her possession, and so on. Assume that agents on the ground could confirm most of this information.

Would you make wise decisions based on accurate interpretations of the satellite images or would you just take a chance and follow your gut feelings alone based on hope? That is just a sneak preview of what God can do for you.

I know a lady who had difficulties of conception. She was very angry at life, and often stated that life was not fair. One day she got pregnant, and was very excited. She carried the baby to term. Upon delivery, it was discovered that her baby was afflicted with a fatal heritable disease.

Where did that disease come from? Somewhere in the family tree of her husband, that recessive disorder had been passing from generation to generation, and showed up in her baby. She had no way of knowing that that disease would afflict her only child. Was God trying to tell her something with her previous miscarriages? You be the judge of that!

There are all types of afflictions that can be transmitted from generation to generation. These are not readily visible to the naked eye. For example, great grand parents could be afflicted with Amyotrophic Lateral Sclerosis (ALS), Multiple Sclerosis, Muscular Dystrophy, Sickle Cell Anemia, and Tay Sac's Disease. These challenges usually originate from alterations in maternal mitochondrial chromosomes. I know a woman who is now dying of ALS. Everything was fine over the preceding 70 or so years. Suddenly, that disease showed up. There is now severe distress in her children. They are wondering which of them could have the same disease. Had she known, she possibly would have taken other decisions during her fruitful years.

Changes do occur in the chromosomes during spermatogenesis or oogenesis, especially past a certain age. These changes among other things could encompass deletions, insertions, inversions, or substitutions. Other genetic changes that include but not limited to non-disjunctions, polyploidy, aneuploidy, and incomplete dominance.

Granted there are several remedial techniques such as genetic screening, gene therapy, in-vitro fertilization, and other surgical procedures available in certain parts of the world. Remember this book is designed to reach a global audience, most of whom do not have insurance coverage or the technology for such procedures available in their countries.

Sometimes even with the advent of modern technologies, complications could occur during delivery or childbirth that might jeopardize the life of both parent and child. For example, some twins are conjoined requiring delicate and complete surgeries to separate.

The point I am trying to make is that, as human, we cannot always tell what, where or why certain things happen or are in store for us.
I know and fully understand that it is in God's power to do all things. Therefore, it would not be unreasonable for one to demand that He provides everything we need in

the manner in which we think. After all, several who do not believe in Him seem to have things their way. But remember, His thoughts are not our thoughts.

Therefore, do not allow failure to consummate a marriage by the procreation of children to become major issues in your marital relations. Rather, you must depend on God to provide you the answers based on faith and acceptance, resting assured that He knows what is best for you and would guide your affairs accordingly. Remember, adoption is always an alternative, and that could be His plan for you!

Let us look at other instances where everything went well with expecting mothers, who delivered normal healthy babies. Sooner or later, we come to the painful realization that life is not always a bed of roses. Why is it that some spouses or children become the target of violence and abuse by certain parents or step parents? I have done my best to provide some of the answers to this question in Chapter 7 of this book. Therefore, I will not belabor this point here.

A large number of studies have shown that divorce has both a short-term and a long-term impact on children. Research also demonstrates that this impact often extends into adult life with consequences for health, family life, educational performance, and occupational status.

In the short term, the age of children affected by divorce can relate to changes in behavior (43).

The most common reactions in children are anger, directed at one or both parents, sadness, and depression. In younger children, clinging to parents and 'regressive' reactions like bedwetting are frequently seen while older children may withdraw somewhat from the home and seek relationships elsewhere.

Furthermore, older children can disengage from the family situation by going out with friends or establishing supportive relationships with older relatives or family friends. Younger children without these opportunities may behave differently.

Conversely, the absence of monitoring by parents and 'over investment' in peer relationships can lead to behavior problems in older children. Researchers (43) have found in their three-wave study that adolescent children in divorced single mother families and in stepfamilies formed through remarriage, consistently scored less well on indices of behavior, competence, and education than comparable children whose parents were stably married.

Experience of divorce, as a child, can have adverse effects in terms of health, behavior and economic status thirty years later. There is evidence that children whose parents divorced when they are less than five years of age are particularly vulnerable. A series of other studies (43) indicate:

- children of divorced parents seem much more susceptible to psychiatric illness.
- alcohol consumption by women whose parents are divorced is far higher than women from intact families.
- the incidence of stomach ulcers and colitis is four times higher for men aged 26 and whose parents had divorced before the child was five years old compared to those who had reached 16 years.
- children of divorce living with formerly married mothers have a 50 per cent greater risk of developing asthma, and a 20-30 per cent greater risk of injury, and
- parental divorce can be a factor in children's longevity.

### Behavioral problem

There is also widespread evidence of increased behavioral problems and delinquency among both boys and girls whose parents have divorced.

Unlike many of their parents, children do not usually experience an immediate sense of relief when their families breakup. Rather, most children undergo a great amount of emotional distress immediately after the divorce as they try to adjust to their new living conditions.

Similarly, children who experienced separation and divorce were two to three times more likely to have been suspended or expelled from school, and three times as likely to be in need of treatment for emotional or behavioral problems.

These children also scored higher on measures of antisocial behavior, anxiety or depression, inattention, hyperactivity, dependency, and fearfulness.

There are numerous references in the literature that linked some violent and aggressive behavior in school-age children to marital and family disruption.

## Youth depression and suicide

Marital disruption has also been implicated in youth depression and suicide as well as early sexual activity.

## Educational performance

A series of studies performed in Australia (43) on the impact of parental divorce on children have found the educational performance of children is adversely affected. Such studies reveal that:

- the adverse educational effects of divorce can occur in children at any age,
- the chances of attending university decrease for children of divorce; and
- unemployment and employment in low-paying jobs is more prevalent among children of divorced parents.

Other studies reveal that children of divorced parents divorce are more likely to drop out of school and less likely to go onto tertiary studies.

## Intergenerational effect

A series of studies have confirmed the intergenerational impact of divorce (43). Twenty-five years after their parents divorce, children continue to suffer the emotional repercussions.

Wallerstein (40, 41) noted that 'it would be hard to find any other group of children except perhaps the victims of a natural disaster who suffered such a rate of serious psychological problems.

The possibility of intergenerational effects of divorce were also revealed in a longitudinal study in the UK. Using data from a cohort of the population that has been followed from birth to age 33, researchers were able to trace the effects of parental divorce on indicators of mental health over the entire sweep of the British study - from age 7 - when behavioral information was first collected, through assessments at ages 11, 16, 23, and 33.

It is known that that much of the apparent effect of a parental divorce on children's emotional problems between ages 7 and 11 could be attributed to characteristics of the child and family prior to the divorce.

### The role of conflict

One characteristic that appears important is conflict between parents. The existence of conflict has been cited as a reason in favor of divorce: better to separate than to inflict a conflict relationship on children (43).

There is reason to suggest that it is parental conflict rather than actual separation that is associated with poor outcomes for children following divorce. This has led some people to suggest that it is better to resolve a high conflict situation by ending the parental relationships than by allowing it to continue.

Of course, we would like to see more effective conflict resolution techniques implemented to salvage troubled marriages. If conflict is allowed to continue without effective intervention, that could lead to family violence.

Some authorities have suggested that the first two years of marriage are critical because that's when the risk of divorce is particularly high (27).

An article written by Kathleen Parrish (26) stated categorically that, " research shows it's not how much you love each other that predicts the success of a marriage, but how you handle the problems that come along in life...Happily married couples view problems as 'us against the problem'. They identify themselves as a team."

Another article written by Carma Wadley (39) provides various tools for predicting success in marriage. An excerpt from that article is presented below.
Let's look first at the factors that predict marital dissatisfaction:

Individual traits
    1. High neurotic traits
    2. Anxiety
    3. Depression

4. Impulsiveness
5. Self-consciousness
6. Vulnerability to stress
7. Anger/hostility
8. Dysfunctional beliefs. If you enter marriage convinced that you live on different planets, or that you'll never understand each other, you probably won't.

Couple traits
1. Dissimilarity
2. Short acquaintanceship
3. Premarital sex (especially a lot of experience with many different partners)
4. Premarital pregnancy
5. Cohabitation
6. Poor communication and conflict-resolution skills

Context
1. Younger age
2. Unhealthy family-of-origin experiences
3. Parental divorces or chronic marital conflict
4. Parental or friends' disapproval
5. Pressure to marry
6. Little education or career preparation

On the other side of the triangle are the leading factors that predict marital satisfaction:

Individual traits
1. High self-esteem
2. Flexibility
3. Assertiveness
4. Sociability

Couple traits
1. Similarity
2. Long acquaintanceship

3. Good communication skills
4. Good conflict resolution skills/style

Context
1. Older age
2. Healthy family-of-origin experiences
3. Happy parental marriage
4. Parental and friends' approval
5. Significant education and career preparation

These, too, are things couples can work on. Research has shown that the better acquainted a couple is, the higher the marital satisfaction. Provided below are suggested ways to test that acquaintanceship:

1. List your partner's five most important life goals
2. Discuss how you well you know your partner with others
3. How does your experience compare with theirs
4. Write a description of how well you know your partner as well as your blind spots
5. Look at how familiar you are with your partner's current life-stressors

If you go through these exercises together, you may learn a lot about each other. Then you can set goals for improvement. And you can do this for each of the traits (39).

Unemployment and other work-related factors contribute significantly to marriage and family breakdown. Unemployment leads to financial hardship, lowers self-esteem, isolation, and limited ability of families to lead fulfilling lives in the community.

On the other hand, some family members work longer hours due to financial pressures and fear of losing employment. That tends to reduce quality time spent by the family.

A recent study by the Creighton University Center for Marriage and Family in the same article suggested that time, sex, and money pose the three largest hindrances to satisfaction in the lives of newly married couples.

The article concluded that debt brought into marriage, the couple's financial situation, balancing job and family, and frequency of sexual relations were of greatest concern to those ages 29 and under.

Those age 30 and over shared with their younger counterparts the concerns of balancing job and family and the frequency of sexual relations, but in addition, they cited constant bickering and expectations about household tasks.
Illness also tends to create destabilizing stresses within families. For example, children with disabilities or chronic or life threatening or psychiatric illness tend to have negative impacts on marital stability.

There are also issues from blended families, where there are children from previous marriages. Couples often lack understanding of the complexity of issues they need to deal with, and thus have unrealistic expectations.

## Blended Families

The number of blended families all over the world is on the rise for obvious reasons. Certainly, adjustment to the new blended family environment should be considered a major challenge for all members of the family. It must be understood that this is probably harder on the affected children than the adult members of the family in view.

The adult members of such families sometimes fail to grasp the signals or body languages that might indicate discontentment for the status quo of their children until it is too late.

What matters most to the adult family members at the time is that they consider themselves deeply in love, wish to live together, and would worry about the impacts of their decision on the children later. They might even expect the children to 'understanding' the decision they have made.

Consequently they fail to factor in an adjustment time for the children in the new environment. Failure to take into account the time for emotional adjustment by the children in a blended family setting could be a potential time bomb under certain circumstances for either parent, if not properly handled.

The fact of the matter is that some children may not desire or appreciate the blended family situation, but may not wish to express their resentment openly for various reasons. Left unaddressed, grave consequences could result under such circumstances.

For example recently, there are various stories in the news about people who allowed their vehicles to slide downhill into water bodies with their vehicle doors locked, and windows up while their children helplessly drowned. Subsequent testimonies revealed the motives behind such hideous crimes, namely, a fiancée, live-in boyfriend/girlfriend or stepparent did not want the children from the previous relationship.

Time and space would not allow me to recount the numerous incidents of rape, incest, or sexual molestation of children or step children which often leave indelible scars on the minds and emotions of the victims for many years thereafter. Often the victims are afraid to share such horrible experiences, or one of the parents finds it appropriate to keep the matter concealed in order to protect the perpetrator or family member.

I am convinced that education on the subject of blended families, coupled with love, perseverance, patience, and time have a way of setting the stage for children in such families to overcome the then and now. Truly, time can do so much. Allow me to share with you a few pointers that might enhance harmony in a blended relationship (9):

- If possible, the newly blended family should relocate into a new home so as to put past memories or reminders to rest as much as possible. I know a blended family in the city where we live. The wife in the blended family is very religious. She accepted her husband's children as her own. They actually refer to her as their 'mom.' In fact, people who do not know about the marital background of her family have often remarked how 'you and your daughter look very much alike!' She had a house prior to the marriage.

However, the family chose to stay in the husband's house because it was in the children's school district, was much bigger and in a more affluent neighborhood. Despite her good intentions, the mere thought that another woman previously inhabited their home was too overpowering for her. Sooner or later, she replaced the entire carpet in the house, then the furniture. Next, she had the house repainted, changed the toilets, and is now putting pressure on the husband to sell the house.

- Continually strive to keep the daily schedule the same in order to maintain continuity. Change usually brings about a fear of the unknown. A major benefit of continuity is that it tends to minimize the impact on the children of the uneasiness or fear associated with change in the family composition.

- Share family time and resources equitably. Naturally, biological children demand more attention from their biological parents. With time, they figure out that they are probably different from the stepchildren. Do not allow yourself to be caught in a 'competition trap' when such children play these little games to instill envy or jealousy in the step children. In certain instances, especially, when the step children exercise their visitation rights, keep what you do with your biological children low key while the stepchildren are away. Children can be very observant, and pick up on such subtle events that might have taken place inadvertently.

- Be yourself. Some stepchildren may remind you, in cases of discipline, that you are not their biological parent. These commonplace statements have wrecked many a marriages. Accept who you are but let the child know that you are the adult in charge, and intend to enforce inbound or out of bounds rules established for the family. There are those who believe discipline should be implemented only by the biological parent. Only in the absence of the biological parent should the stepparent step in. I disagree with that opinion. When two people get married, they must be as ONE. That is the major focus of this book, and the intention of God for the marriage institution. Of course, I trust that the biological parent can discern between discipline and child abuse. Hopefully, that would not be the case. In certain

African cultures, it is the role of the male figure of the household to discipline children of the family. In the absence of the biological male parent, other male figures in the household assume that responsibility. Only in the absence of a male figure are females allowed to discipline children of the family.

- The parents should be supportive of each other in the implementation of discipline in the household. Major troubles start when one parent feels there are 'untouchables' in the family. Or there is resentment from the other parent when the other parent implements discipline. The two have now become as ONE. They should have discussed this item before getting married.

- It is a natural reaction for children to maintain an affection or loyalty to their biological parent. Do not be offended by that. Be mindful that feelings of love and hate by stepchildren may change frequently.

  I know that in certain parts of the world, not all members of the family sit together to eat at the dinner table. I am also aware that sometimes because of work schedule changes it is not possible for all member of a given family to eat together. In general, however, most families do. This can be an excruciating time for children of a blended family because it reminds them of the way it was with their biological parents. Stepparents should strive to make this valuable time as peaceful as possible, and allow time for readjustment to take its course.

- Get involved in your stepchildren's activities. Volunteering in their extra-curricular activities, picking them up from the day care center or driving them to school usually work well in creating family identity.

- Maintain the privacy of the marital relationship. A healthy stepfamily relationship is based on a strong marital relationship. Blending a family takes time and patience to cultivate. Think of a successful farmer in your region. First, the farmer clears and tills the land. Next, the farmer sows seeds or transplants seedlings. At the appropriate time, there is application of pre-emergence fertilizers, post- emergence fertilizer, herbicides, and other farm events. The farmer waits patiently for the rains, or irrigates the field in hope of a great harvest. The investment finally pays off in a great harvest. For that reason, you must learn too.

- Be patient, persevere, and pray. There will be difficulties in the initial stages. Remember, if you as a stepparent, falter rapidly to consider divorce at the onset of initial resistance, then your strength is small. Those who patiently persevere and wait for time to heal will eventually earn the love, respect, and crown of glory for their families.

Furthermore, in the wake of the women's liberation movement, women now have a radically new view of their role and status in society and many men are uncertain how to respond to this change.

Another interesting outcome reported in Carma Wadley's article was that what couple argued about was not as important as how they argued. This demonstrates the level of their respect for each other. Other less major reasons for family breakdowns included cruelty, especially in India, and snoring in both Russia and Britain.

Finally, the articles reported that there was a 'peak marriage age' in the mid-twenties. People who got married between the ages of 23-27 were much less likely to get divorced than those who married in their teens.

## Factors that Could Crumble Marital and Family Relationships

After an extensive review of available literature, it was apparent that the following factors (4, 48) for the most part summarize the most common reasons for divorce in most communities:

- Financial issues
- Lack of commitment to the marriage

- Drastic change in priorities
- Infidelity
- Failed expectations or unmet needs
- Addictions and substance abuse-these include drugs, alcohol, and gambling. Left unchecked, these issues usually lead to domestic violence.
- Physical, sexual or emotional abuse and lack of conflict resolution skills, and
- Poor communication

## Communication

Because of the importance of communication, and by popular request from the people I interviewed while preparing the manuscript on this subject, I would like to further expound on this element.

Poor communications-this situation arises when family members fail to communicate effectively with each other. Effective communication is the ability to be understood rather than the skill with which points are made. It is reinforced by mutual trust. Trust takes time to cultivate; yet it provides a forum for intimate discussions. Suggested below is a generalized outline to accomplish effective communications in relationships:

1. Be sure to ask questions during your discussions. This would ensure you understand your mate's perspectives. In this regard, take time to choose your words very carefully. They must portray the essence of your thought process or rationale. Additional words of wisdom could be found in the book of Proverbs.
2. Be a good listener. It has been stated that a major reason why human being has two ears but only one mouth is for us to listen more and speak less. Being a good listener allows us to better appreciate our spouse's perspectives. Good listening skills encompass but are not limited to, empathizing with our spouse, attentiveness, not being judgmental, and not interrupting while our spouse is speaking.
3. Listen carefully to your spouse's feelings by being very observant. Do not be accusative or insensitive.
4. Be sure to discuss any issues of concern directly with your spouse, not others, as soon as it happens. As stated in the scriptures, "Do not let the sun go down on your wrath!"
5. Be humble. Be the one who initiates resolution of the conflict. That shows a sign of strength rather than weakness.
6. Step back and look at the bigger picture
7. Remember, there is no challenge that cannot be surmounted with Love!!!

The above information has been presented in a format that relates to first time marriages, even though the preceding concepts could be applicable in either situation. Available statistics suggest that the number of blended families is on the rise all over the world. For that reason, I must devote this segment specifically to provide insights that might help strengthen such relationships.

In addition, **spiritual or physiological** factors might lead to a breakdown in the marital or family relationship. Physiological factors refer specifically to the 'changes of Life', that is andropause and menopause which underlie the so-called 'middle-age crisis'.

Spiritual factors.

Not all relationship breakdowns emanate from differences between personalities. Neither do they always arise from the preceding factors. Sometimes they might originate from external influences that may be physical or spiritual. Since I have already discussed several of the physical factors, let us focus our attention on a lesser-known culprit that can be equally as devastating to a marriage.

The existence and operation of spiritual forces can sometimes have very negative impacts on a marital relationship. This factor is much more prevalent in certain parts of the world than at others. Nevertheless, it must be discussed at this point because of to the global outreach of this book.

Some family members, especially those who experience rejection, inferiority, or insecurity, or those who are curious or desire to know about the great mysteries of life, easily get lured into occult practices that open spiritual doors for familiar spirits to enter and wreck their relationship. Provided below is a brief summary of some of these practices that could have very adverse impacts on marriages:

- Necromancy or communication with the dead.
- Divination which is an attempt to discern future events or to discover that which cannot be known by normal means. It includes occult practices, spirit mediums, witchcraft, voodoo priests, medicine men, and shamans.

These so-called spirits will stand on either side of the male or female causing all kinds of trouble in their marriage. There are vicious sexual spirits which can molest and torment susceptible individuals. Those attacking females are called Incubus and those concentrating on males are called succubus. They often come into prominence in connection with witchcraft spells, love potion, and other curses of lust.

These curses of lust can also operate when people consciously or habitually experiment with sexual sin. For example, having a sexual relationship out of wedlock, or conceiving a child during the courtship and becoming a single parent. This illegitimate or bastard child goes under the curse for several generations.

Spirits commonly found in the "bastard" include lust, sadism, masochism, sex goddess, such as of the female body (Venus worship), worship of the male body (phallic worship), nudity, nakedness, pornography, rebellion and rejection.

Those inherited in witchcraft cause some of the worst problems, because they begin their work even on very young children.

Such spirits delight in inflicting pain, fear, nighttime fears, restless nights, insomnia, pressure sleep, nightmares, tormented dreams, blockage in family relationships, damage to the family structure, family destruction, family disunity, separation from family, hurt feelings, miscommunication, lack of communication, destructive lust, impotence in husbands, fear of sex in marriage or frigidity in wives, gynecological disorders, dissatisfaction, frustration, desolation, defilement, immorality, free love, sexual curiosity, abnormal adolescence, lewdness, sexual impurity, sex perversion of all kinds, rape, assault, abuse, child molestation, sexual desire for children (pedophilia), uncleanness, seduction, abnormal sensitivity, lasciviousness, occult sex, uncontrolled sex, incubi, succubi, lesbian spirits, homosexuality spirits, bisexuality, promiscuity, adultery, prostitution, harlotry, fornication, sexual fantasies, cruelty, nudity, pornography, sex with animals, anal sex, sadism, masochism, incest (having unlawful sex with close relative like father, mother, sister, brother, uncle aunt), filthy dreams, filthy conversation, shame, condemnation, guilt, depression, suicide, sorrow, hopelessness, unhappiness, bitter disappointment, rebellion, all kinds of rejection, confusion, shame, anger, failure, arrested development in body, mind, will and emotions.

Satan's emissaries work constantly to control the individual by disrupting this three part harmony causing stunted growth in body, strong emotions and mental anguish on their victims (18).

The Lord created man as body, soul (mind, will, emotions) and spirit. If the devil can slip in undetected in one area of a person's life he will continue to spread his rottenness to other areas. This makes it imperative that we learn to detect these dangerous inroads early; prevent, and root them out.

These depraved spirits play with their captives, cruelly tormenting and using their bodies to satisfy the orgiastic and filthy cravings of the demons. Once the spirits entered the bodies, they do not care whether or not the experience is pleasant for their host. They rather prefer to produce pain and suffering.

This way they not only enjoy the lust they generate but also the horror with which the cringing and helpless person is filled. Again and again, he is driven to do what he has come to hate and dread. The lower the person can be made to sink, the more animalistic and sickeningly filthy he becomes, the more the demons enjoy their cruel game.

A person can expect to be invaded by demonic spirits if he/she dabbles with psychic phenomena profanities such as fortune telling, sorcery, calling spirits, witchcraft, or any kind of occult. As his/her defenses drop by his/her meddling curiosity, occult spirits can and will enter in and establish themselves. These are the spirits that travel to the third and fourth generations through the parents by inheritance, because consorting with them breaks the first commandment by contacting another god.

- Transcendental meditation. Transcendental meditation, coupled with chanting of mantras, opens a person direct to demonic beings operating in the spirit realm.
- Imaginary playmates. The playmate may be invisible to others but visible to a child. He or she becomes a companion and teacher to the child.

The other component that could negatively impact marital relation is physiological. I am specifically referring to andropause and menopause!

# CHAPTER 6

## Menopause and Andropause

Some people do not like to discuss the manifestations or impacts of physiological changes in their lives. They consider them too 'personal.' However, if these are not properly understood and handled, they could have devastating effects on a marital relationship. Physiological changes play significant roles in middle-age crises and divorce.

People often wonder what went wrong when they learn of divorce between middle-age couples. One would expect that after 20 or 30 years of marriage, a couple should know and understand each other well enough to surmount most of the issues in their relationship. But that is not always the case. Physiological factors become more pronounced around middle-age. Such changes could not only lead to middle-age crisis and divorce. They could actually send certain innocent spouses to their early death. Therefore, it is important to discuss these topics here.

As a motivational speaker, I was invited to give a presentation to a group of people not too long ago on these issues. After the presentation, a lady probably in her middle forties stopped by to congratulate me while a gentleman stood impatiently behind her. He whispered to that lady it was time for them to leave.

I sensed something was amiss. Instinctively, I handed my business card to that lady so I could attend to the other who waited in line to shake my hand. Several months later, I got an email message from her.

I later learned that the gentleman who stood behind her was, in fact, her husband. That lady experienced early signs of menopause. Her husband misinterpreted her symptoms, and suspected she was having extra-marital relations.

As sometimes occurs in life, he opted to 'show her that two can play the game.' He engaged in an adulterous relationship with a younger woman, who incidentally and unknowingly was afflicted by the HIV/AIDS virus. He became infected, and passed on that deadly virus to his wife. They were both dying of AIDS. She pleaded with me in her communication not to give up on what I was doing to help prevent future innocent deaths.

That was an overwhelming reason why I would like to place these physiological factors on your minds so that you can discuss them in the privacy of your homes. Therefore, relax, pay attention, and get ready for a brief lesson on andropause and menopause.

Let me emphasize that the information I am about to present in this chapter is intended to increase the readers knowledge and understanding of menopause and andropause. **It should not be considered medical advice.** If you are experiencing any of the signs and symptoms described in this book, I will encourage you to discuss such issues with your family doctor for more appropriate treatment or intervention.

Stedman's Medical Dictionary (46) defines menopause as the permanent cessation of the menses. This condition may be diagnosed in retrospect when one year has passed since the last menses.

The average age of menopause is 51. However, menopause that starts at the age of 36-40 is considered normal.

Perimenopause is defined as the transitional period from normal menstrual periods to no periods at all. The transition can, and usually does, take up to ten years. During the perimenopausal transition you may experience a combination of PMS and menopausal symptoms or no symptoms at all. PMS, on the other hand, can occur at any age but is more common at age 30's and 40's.

The age your mother or older sister began menopause can have a bearing on when you will begin menopause. If your mother went through menopause in her late 40's and you're 34 it is most likely PMS. If your mother suffered from PMS then you are more likely to suffer as well. However, your mother might not remember when she went through menopause and your older sister may not admit to it. The only other reliable factor is if you smoke.

If you smoke, you can count on menopause starting 1-2 years earlier than if you don't. Some of the symptoms of depression are found in both PMS and perimenopause. After reviewing your family history for age of menopause and occurrence of PMS and depression, you should complete a symptom diary or calendar. This will be a unique record of your feelings on a daily basis.

In the week before your period emotional symptoms will increase and physical symptoms may begin. In the last few days, emotional symptoms will peak and then rapidly disappear after your menses start. There are variations of this pattern, but the key is symptoms that increase before and are relieved after your period.

If your menses are occurring sooner than 21 days it may be perimenopause or a more serious gynecological condition and you need to be evaluated by your health care provider. Menses occurring later than 45 days are more consistent with menopause or perimenopause. If physical symptoms predominate, especially hot flashes, vaginal dryness and night sweats, and if they last throughout the month unrelated to menses, think more about menopause.

Remember, menopause before the age of 40 is called premature menopause, and is rare. However, perimenopause can begin before age 40. Surgical removal of the ovaries is the most common cause of premature menopause. Until you are firmly in menopause, that is, no periods for one year, you can still get pregnant (44). Physical signs include but may not be limited to:

- Irregular periods (changes in frequency, duration, skipped periods, etc.)
- Infertility
- Hot flashes and night sweats
- Vaginal dryness
- Bladder control problems
- Insomnia/disrupted sleep
- Palpitations
- Weight gain (especially around your waist and abdomen)
- Skin changes (dryness, thinning look)
- Headaches

- Breast tenderness
- Gastrointestinal distress and nausea.
- Tingling or itchy skin.
- "Buzzing" in your head, electric shock sensation
- Bloating
- Dizziness/lightheadedness
- Sore joints/muscles
- Hair loss or thinning
- Increase in facial hair
- Changes in body odor
- Dry Mouth and other oral symptoms

Emotional signs may also include but not limited to:

- Irritability
- Mood swings
- Lowered libido
- Anxiety
- "Brain fog" -- difficulty concentrating, confusion
- Memory lapses
- Extreme fatigue/low energy levels
- Confusion/lack of concentration
- Feeling emotionally detached

Recently, it has been suggested that up to two-thirds of the women with premature ovarian failure have it due to:

- An autoimmune disorder.
- Chromosomal irregularity
- Oophorectomy and total hysterectomy
  This is one of the most common causes of early menopause In this case, women experience premature menopause after removal of both of the ovaries (a bilateral oophorectomy) or removal of the uterus, both fallopian tubes, and both ovaries (a total hysterectomy). Because both of your

ovaries are removed, your estrogen and progesterone levels plunge, leading immediately to menopause.

- Ovarian damage due to other surgical procedures
- Radiation therapy and/or chemotherapy
  With the rise in cancer treatments has come a rise in premature menopause due to these treatments. Unfortunately, the significant doses of radiation or chemotherapy used to kill cancer can also damage the ovaries, resulting in premature menopause.
- Tamoxifen
  Tamoxifen used to be prescribed after having been diagnosed for breast cancer
- Family History
  It's not a hard-and-fast rule, but most women go through menopause at about the same age their mothers did.
- Viral Infections
  If your mother contracts a viral infection while you're still in her uterus, it can affect your ovarian development, causing you to be born with lower number of eggs than you otherwise would have had. In this case, since you start with fewer eggs than most women, you run out of eggs more quickly, which may result in premature menopause.

Other disorders

- Thyroid Disease: Both hypothyroid and hyperthyroid often cause symptoms that mimic those you get when your hormone levels drop. This is particularly true of hypothyroid which can cause hair loss, weight gain, moodiness (the "blahs"); and amenorrhea the stopping of periods. Hyperthyroid can cause palpitations and sweats (that may seem like either hot flashes or night sweats). In both cases, though, proper diagnosis and treatment will result in the reversal of symptoms

- Hyperprolactinemia: This is a disease that is marked by overproduction of *prolactin* the hormone that is responsible for milk production in your breasts. Often women with hyperprolactinemia also go through amenorrhea the stopping of menstrual periods.
- Pituitary and/or Hypothalamic Disorders: Often women with pituitary disorders (such as hypothalamic or pituitary failure or pituitary tumors) go through amenorrhea.
- Cushing's disease: This occurs when adrenal glands are overactive resulting in amenorrhea.
- Polycystic Ovarian Syndrome (PCOS): Also known as polycystic ovarian disease (PCOD), this can cause skipped periods and a number of other symptoms, including excessive hair growth.

Other causes of amenorrhea (stopped periods) include:

- excessive weight gain or weight loss
- use of certain drugs (such as phenothiazines which are psychiatric drugs; and certain narcotics)
- excessive exercise
- recent use of birth control pills (it is not uncommon to stop getting periods for up to six months after discontinuing the pill.

Menopause (46,47) is a normal change in a woman's life when her period stops. That's why some people call it menopause "the change of life." During menopause, a woman's body slowly makes less of the hormones estrogen and progesterone. This often happens between the ages of 45 and 55 years old. A woman has reached menopause when she has not had a period for 12 months in a row (and there are no other causes for this change).

Symptoms of menopause may include but not limited to:

- Changes in your period – the time between periods and the flow from month to month may be different.
- Abnormal bleeding or "spotting" – common as you near menopause.

- Hot flashes ("hot flushes") – getting warm in the face, neck and chest.
- Night sweats and sleeping problems – these may lead to feeling tired, stressed, or tense.
- Vaginal changes – the vagina may become dry and thin, and sex and vaginal exams may be painful. You also might get more vaginal infections.
- Thinning of your bones – this may lead to loss of height and bone breaks (osteoporosis).
- Mood changes – such as mood swings, depression, and irritability.
- Urinary problems – such as leaking, burning or pain when urinating, or leaking when sneezing, coughing, or laughing.
- Problems with concentration or memory.
- Less interest in sex and changes in sexual response.
- Weight gain or increase in body fat around the waist.
- Hair thinning or loss.

Sometimes, younger women need a hysterectomy (surgery to remove the uterus and ovaries) to treat health problems such as endometriosis or cancer. After surgery, you will enter into what is known as induced or surgical menopause. This is menopause that happens to your body right away, and it is brought on by the surgery.

You will no longer have periods. Since your ovaries will be removed, you may have many menopausal symptoms right away, instead of gradually. You can talk with your doctor about how to best manage these symptoms.

Women who have undergone hysterectomy but have their ovaries left in place will not have induced menopause because their ovaries will continue to make hormones. But, because their uterus is removed, they no longer have their periods and they cannot bear children. They also might have hot flashes since the surgery can sometimes disturb the blood supply to the ovaries. Later on, they also might have natural menopause a year or two earlier than expected.

The term postmenopause refers to all the years beyond menopause. It is the period past the time at which you have not had a period for 12 months in a row — whether your menopause was natural or induced.

Many women in perimenopause and menopause feel depressed and irritable. Some researchers believe that the decrease in estrogen triggers changes in the brain, causing depression. Others think that other symptoms being experienced, such as sleep problems, hot flashes, night sweats, and fatigue causes these feelings. Or, it could be a combination of hormone changes and symptoms.

Treatment for such symptoms should be arranged between the patient and her doctor.

Changes in bleeding are normal as you near menopause. There are also other common causes of bleeding in the years after menopause. The decline in your body's estrogen levels can cause tissues lining the vagina to become thin, dry, and less elastic. Sometimes this lining can become broken or easily inflamed and bleed.

It can also become injured during sex or even during a pelvic exam. Once you've reached menopause, though, you should report any bleeding that you have to your doctor. Uterine bleeding after menopause could be a sign of other health problems. Other things that can cause abnormal bleeding include:

- fibroids
- the use of birth control pills
- a hormonal imbalance
- non-cancerous growths in the lining of the uterus

For some women, many of their menopause symptoms will go away over time without treatment. Other women will choose treatment for their symptoms and to prevent bone loss that can happen near menopause. Treatments may include prescription drugs that contain types of hormones that your ovaries stop making around the time of menopause. Hormone therapy can contain estrogen alone or estrogen with progestin (for a woman who still has her uterus or womb).

Hormone therapy can help with menopause by:

- reducing hot flashes

- treating vaginal dryness
- slowing bone loss
- decreasing mood swings and depression

DO NOT use hormone therapy to prevent heart attacks, strokes, memory loss or Alzheimer's disease. Remember there also are other medicines that can help your bones. For some women, hormone therapy may increase their chance of getting:

- blood clots
- heart attacks
- strokes
- breast cancer
- gall bladder disease

Some women decide to take herbal, natural, or plant-based products to help their symptoms. Some of the most common ones are:

- Soy. This contains *phytoestrogens* (estrogen-like substances from a plant). But, there is no proof that soy–or other sources of phytoestrogens–really do relieve hot flashes

- Other sources of phytoestrogens. These include herbs such as black cohosh, a member of the buttercup family, wild yam, dong quai, and valerian root.

- Bioidentical hormone therapy. Some women visit *alternative medicine* doctors and get a prescription for these products, which are made from different plant hormones that are like those in a woman's body. Each prescription is hand-mixed, and the dose can vary from patient to patient.

- Hot Flashes. A hot environment, eating or drinking hot or spicy foods, alcohol, or caffeine, and stress can bring on hot flashes. Try to avoid these triggers. Dress in layers and keep a fan in your home or workplace. Regular exercise might also bring relief from hot flashes and other symptoms. Ask

- your doctor about taking an antidepressant medicine. There is proof that these can be helpful for some women.

- Vaginal Dryness. Use an over-the-counter vaginal lubricant. There are also prescription estrogen replacement creams that your doctor might give you. If you have spotting or bleeding while using estrogen creams, you should see your doctor.

- Problems Sleeping. One of the best ways to get a good night's sleep is to get at least 30 minutes of physical activity on most days of the week. But, avoid a lot of exercise close to bedtime. Also avoid alcohol, caffeine, large meals, and working right before bedtime. You might want to drink something warm, such as herb tea or warm milk, before bedtime. Try to keep your bedroom at a comfortable temperature. Avoid napping during the day and try to go to bed and get up at the same times every day.

- Memory problems. Ask your doctor about mental exercises you can do to improve your memory. Try to get enough sleep and be physically active.

- Mood swings. Try to get enough sleep and be physically active. Ask your doctor about relaxation exercises you can do. Ask your doctor about taking an antidepressant medicine. There is proof that these can be helpful. Think about going to a support group for women who are going through the same thing as you, or getting counseling to talk through your problems and fears.

You can use this chart to keep track of menopausal symptoms that bother you. Take it with you when you visit your doctor, so you both can figure out the best way to handle them.

| Date | Symptoms | Things I've tried to help them | Questions for my doctor | New things to try |
|------|----------|-------------------------------|------------------------|-------------------|
|      |          |                               |                        |                   |
|      |          |                               |                        |                   |
|      |          |                               |                        |                   |
|      |          |                               |                        |                   |
|      |          |                               |                        |                   |
|      |          |                               |                        |                   |
|      |          |                               |                        |                   |
|      |          |                               |                        |                   |
|      |          |                               |                        |                   |

# Andropause

"Midlife crisis" is often the transitional period for men when they experience what is termed as the "second childhood". This period usually starts from age 40 to 45 (45). It is also called Andropause because its symptoms coincide with the decrease in a class of male hormones called androgen.

All men are affected by these symptoms, although some to a larger degree than others.

## Symptoms of Andropause

- Diminished libido
- Reduced frequency of sex (the "senior slump")
- Erectile dysfunction
- Infertility
- Changes in body composition
- Reductions in body and facial hair
- Osteoporosis. Andropause is in effect the reverse of puberty.
- Levels of anger
- Confusion
- Depression, and
- Fatigue that is significantly higher than those reported by men with normal testosterone levels. The average human male begins to feel some symptoms of Andropause after 40 to 45 years old.

Some of these symptoms could be attributed to a decrease in testosterone levels, including sexual dysfunction.

Other important hormones that have reduced production levels from age 30 onwards include Human Growth Hormone, Melatonin, DHEA, and Pregnenolone.

Consult your doctor for appropriate treatment of these symptoms.

# CHAPTER 7

## Family Violence

As we shall see in this chapter, family violence is a global venomous canker, a social anathema to harmonious marital and family relationship. It must be brought out of the family closet and dealt with head on.

When two people get married, they expect to live happily ever after. Their dreams of having that wonderful companion who would sweep them off their feet have finally come true. If they are believers in the plan outlined in this book, then their ultimate hope is to become 'one flesh.'

However, certain extenuating circumstances sometimes get into the relationship which, if left unchecked, could lead to grave consequences such as family violence. This is related to relationship stress. To reiterate, the focal point for writing this book is to save marriages and strengthen family relationships.

Because of the rampant nature of this social ill, the reader should keep the following information at the backs of their minds, and make it a point to manage relationship stress. Potentially deadly consequences could result from a relationship that is meant to bring joy and happiness to the married couple.

Family violence can be defined as the intentional intimidation or abuse of children, adults or elders by a family member, intimate partner or caretaker to gain power and control over the victim (12). It crosses all socioeconomic lines regardless of race, age, culture or sexual orientation.

Abuse has many forms that include physical and sexual assault, emotional or psychological mistreatment, threats and intimidation, economic abuse and violation of individual rights.

I would like to make the reader aware that several factors contribute to violent behavior in a marital relationship, including but not limited to:

- Biological factors
- Environment in which children are raised. It is known that children who grow up in violent homes are more likely to become victims or perpetrators of family violence in adulthood.
- The presence of violence or neglect in one's family of origin.
- The lack of effective parenting by caregivers.
- The prevalence of violence in society and the media.
- The absence of positive role models to demonstrate and teach nonviolent conflict resolution.
- Socio-economic status. The young, the poor, minorities, divorced, separated, and singles are most likely to experience domestic violence and abuse.
- Gender. Available statistics in the United States show that black females experience domestic violence at a rate 35% higher than that of white females. Furthermore, black males experienced domestic violence at a rate about 62% higher than that of white males and about 22 times the rate of men of other races.
- Unequal power in the relationship.
- Television. The American media portray family and community violence as commonplace.
- Firearm violence. It is widely believed that the prevalence of firearms in American society increases the risk of deadliness in family and community violence.

President George W. Bush, in one of his speeches, considers domestic violence a very serious crime affecting women, men, and children of all backgrounds in the United States. According to the National Crime Victimization Survey, there were nearly 700,000 documented incidents of domestic violence affecting individuals and families in 2001. President Bush is committed to preventing domestic violence, addressing the effects of domestic violence on all Americans, and has secured historic levels of funding for the violence against women programs at the Department of Justice (10).

Domestic violence occurs in one in four American families. Annually, in the United States, an intimate partner abuses 2 to 4 million women each year. Of those, 2,000 to 4,000 die of their injuries.

Until recently, family violence has been considered a private affair. It is now recognized as a widespread social and medical problem. It can result in physical injury, emotional and psychological harm, encompassing substance abuse, depression, suicide, anxiety, bodily disorders, eating disorders and chronic pain.

Family violence affects at least one third of the patients cared for by family physicians. It has been reported that family violence accounts for at least 21,000 hospitalizations: 99,800 hospital days, 28,700 emergency department visits, and 39,000 physicians visits each year (10).

The cost of this social anathema permeates not only the family unit. It imposes great financial burdens on taxpayers. For example, in 1990, the US Department of Justice estimated the aggregate cost of domestic violence to be $67 billion per year. Losses due to child abuse were also estimated to cost the United States government over $164 billion per year.

More than half of these crimes have been committed against women in the process of separation or divorce. In the state of Florida, the figure is even higher (60%). Her current or former spouse did one in three murdered women in.

The problem of Family Violence is not limited to the United States alone. International statistics show that assault of female partners is a worldwide problem. Surveys in various developing countries report the percentage of women experiencing violence in their current relationship as being somewhere between 16% and 67%.

These unfortunate situations could be ameliorated significantly through public education. Recently President George W. Bush signed the 'Violence Against Women Act'.

I hope this act serves as a model for other nations where family violence continues to persist. It is in the best interest of the citizens and government of every nation to address this issue head-on because of the great rewards associated with reduced family violence.

In California, the numbers are equally disheartening. The Department of Justice reports more than 600 incidents of domestic violence every day. In addition, 57 percent of homeless women list domestic violence as the immediate cause of their homelessness.

Western Australian police records suggest an annual incident e of 109 assaults per 100,000 be males on females and 13 per 100,000 be females on males.

Domestic violence is not only directed by men toward women. In less than 5 percent of cases, women do assault male partners. Studies have shown that in the United States, their wives or girlfriends kill 12 percent of murdered men. Most of these cases involve women defending themselves in violent relationships.

Many incidents of family violence do not get reported to appropriate authorities for the following reasons:

- People who have been abused particularly by those close to them may fear that reporting abuse might further threaten their well-being, or that taking action will have no positive effect.
- Power inequity within the relationship.
- Lack of access to assistance, and
- Feelings of shame or embarrassment.

Men are more likely than women to use physical force against a partner. On the other hand, women are more likely to use a weapon, possibly in an attempt to offset differences in strength.

Weapon used in spousal homicide presents a different picture. Men to kill their wives use firearms more often; knives and sharp instruments are relied on more by females to kill their husbands.

There appears to be a glimmer of hope for family violence. Intimate partner violence against women declined by half between 1993 (1.1 million nonfatal cases) and 2001 (588,490) - from 9.8 to 5 per thousand women. Similarly, intimate partner violence against men also declined from 162,870 (1993) to 103,220 (2001) - from 1.6 to 0.9 per thousand males.

Overall, the incidence of such crimes dropped from 5.8 to 3.0 per thousand. Still, 1247 an intimate partner in the United States murdered women and 440 men in 2000.
The comparative figures in 1976 were 1357 men and 1600 women. It declined to around 1300 in 1993. So, while the number overall intimate partner crimes directed at women declined sharply, the number of fatal incidents remained stable since 1993.

Some people choose to live together for a variety of reasons. These so-called 'common law' relationships are not exempt from family violence. The pattern of interaction in abusive dating relationships often resembles the cycle of violence commonly observed in cohabiting intimate relationships.

It is important that the reader pays attention to the following characteristics, even in advance of entering into a marital relationship. It is a vicious cycle characterized by:

1. tension- building phase, followed by
2. an explosive outburst of anger, abusive behavior and/or violence, culminating in
3. a "honeymoon" period marked by contrition on the part of the abusive partner and willingness, whether passive or active, of the abused individual to "kiss and make up".

This pattern may be repeated indefinitely.

A number of warning signs may be present early in a relationship, signs that indicate possibility of danger. The reader is encouraged to pay close attention to these signs. Such signs include but may not be limited to the following:

- When an individual issues threats of violence,
- Is highly jealous or possessive,
- Exerts dominance and control,
- Has been abusive with previous partners, and/or
- Accepts or defends the use of violence, he or she is more prone to escalate these behaviors into violence in his or her relationships.

For this reason, family violence is not just a women's issue. Rather, it must be considered a community problem that needs men and women working together to eradicate this cankerworm from our society.

The good news is that it can be done. It might take years to accomplish. However, with God on our side, we can do it. We have got to start somewhere first, in order to make progress in the right direction. The place to start is to follow the plan outlined in this book!

Family violence by definition involves relationship stress. These deplorable occurrences could be minimized to a great extent through public education. This situation has become so serious, especially in the United States that recently President George W. Bush signed the 'Violence against Women Act'.

I hope this serves as a model for other nations where family violence continues to persist. It is in the best interest of the citizens, and government of every nation to address this issue head-on because of the great rewards associated with reduced family violence.

Marriage brings benefits to adults. Extensive research shows that married adults are happier, are more productive on the job, earn more, have better physical and mental health, and live longer than their unmarried counterparts. Marriage also brings safety to women: Mothers who have married are half has likely to suffer from domestic violence, as are never-married mothers.

Esta Soler (36), president, Family Violence Prevention Fund, recently commented on President Bush signing the Violence against Women Act:

"Our homes and communities in the United States will be safer and healthier because of this Act. We commend Congress for passing this critical legislation, and the President for signing it so promptly. It can significantly improve the nation's response to domestic, sexual and dating violence, and stalking."

A study was conducted by the World Health Organization (WHO) in collaboration with the London School of Hygiene and Tropical Medicine and PATH, a global health organization that interviewed 24,000 women in 15 sites in ten countries that were deemed a representative sample: Bangladesh, Brazil, Ethiopia, Japan, Namibia, Peru, Samoa, Serbia and Montenegro, United Republic of Tanzania and Thailand. (25)

"They found that one quarter to one half of women who were physically assaulted by their partners suffered physical injuries as a result. Abused women were twice as likely as women who were not victims of violence to have poor health and physical and mental health problems, even if the violence occurred many years ago. One in eleven victims of abuse by their partners said they had attempted suicide.

"In most countries studied, four to 12 percent of women who had been pregnant reported having been beaten during pregnancy. More than half of these women had been kicked or punched in the abdomen during pregnancy. Women who reported physical or sexual violence by a partner were also more likely to report having had at least one induced abortion or miscarriage than women who did not report abuse.

"This study shows that women are more at risk from violence at home than in the street," said Dr. LEE Jong-wook, Director-General of WHO. "It also shows how important it is to shine a spotlight on domestic violence globally and to treat it as a major public health issue. Challenging the social norms that condone and therefore perpetuate violence against women is a responsibility for us all."

"At least one in five women reporting physical abuse in the study had never before told anyone about it, with very few seeking help from health care providers, law enforcement or other authorities. Women were more likely to talk to family members or friends.

"The report recommends a range of urgent actions to change attitudes and challenge the norms and inequities that perpetuate abuse. They include training health care providers to identify victims of violence and respond appropriately, raising awareness of the problem, prioritizing the prevention of child sexual abuse, making schools safe for girls, and integrating violence prevention into HIV/AIDS and reproductive health programs."

They found that one quarter to one half of women who were physically assaulted by their partners suffered physical injuries as a result. Abused women were twice as likely as women who were not victims of violence to have poor health and physical and mental health problems, even if the violence occurred many years ago. One in eleven victims of abuse by their partners said they had attempted suicide.

Nearly one in three women will be a victim of domestic violence in her lifetime, according to the Family Violence Prevention Fund. The group also reports that 3 million to 10 million children witness domestic violence every year, as well as that one in five high school girls experience dating violence.

Compounding the real-world consequences for victims of violence and their families, significant economic consequences burden our community as well. Although it is difficult to attach a price tag to the physical and psychological effects of domestic violence, the American Institute on Domestic Violence estimates that domestic violence costs businesses between $3 billion and $5 billion a year in absenteeism, medical costs, employee turnover and lost productivity. That is in addition to the costs associated with the necessary services that victims of domestic violence require.

In the Bay Area of the west coast of the United States, the organization has many dedicated advocates and volunteers, including Community Overcoming Relationship Abuse in San Mateo County, who help deal with the consequences of violence against women.

Men are not naturally inclined toward violence, but young men and boys will learn the behavior if it is part of their home life. Without men speaking out against violence against women, we allow for a society that perpetuates sexism and accepts domestic violence and relationship abuse.

Family violence is not just a women's issue; it's a community problem that needs men and women working together. The White Ribbon Campaign is a meaningful way for men to help create a society free from violence against women.

Although it is impossible to accurately measure family violence, various studies and statistics reveal a considerable problem. In Australia 0.7 per cent of adult women had been victims of assault or threatened at their home.

Western Australian police records suggest an annual incident e of 109 assaults per 100,000 be males on females and 13 per 100,000 be females on males.

When applied to the nation, the survey *Women's Safety*, suggested that 490,000 women (7.1 per cent) had experienced an incident of violence. It indicated that 429,000 women (6.2 per cent) had experienced violence by a man and 110,700 by a woman (1.6 per cent), and 33 per cent of women who experienced violence in the previous 12 months reported incidents by more than one perpetrator. Violence was defined in the survey as any incident involving the occurrence, attempt or threat of either physical or sexual assault.

The National Committee on Violence claims that domestic violence is the most common form of abuse in Australia. According to the National Homicide Monitoring Program, 'just less than one-half of all female victims of homicide were killed whether directly or indirectly as a result of a dispute between intimate partners.'

I have attempted to rekindle the flickering flames of elements that could crumble healthy marital and family relationships. I have also felt lead by the Holy Spirit to encourage the reader to pursue possible ways to rise above these challenges.

I must now focus the reader's attention to additional ways to promote healthy marital and family relation, as well as motivate and inspire the reader on techniques to strengthen the family unit.

Finally, I would like to pique the reader's imagination to certain truths revealed to me by the Holy Spirit regarding how to achieve the goals, objectives, and theme of God's desire and plan for a more abundant, healthier, and happier marital and family relationship. Here, in the next chapter, is how it unfolds.

# CHAPTER 8

## Promoting a Healthy Marital Relationship

I am happy to discover that the institution of marriage is beginning to get the boost it rightfully deserves, even in government circles. The beneficial effects of marriage on individuals and society are beyond reasonable dispute, and there is a broad and growing consensus that government policy should promote rather than discourage healthy marriage (31).

In response to these trends, President George W. Bush has proposed, as part of welfare reform reauthorization, the creation of a pilot program to promote healthy and stable marriage. Participation in the program would be strictly voluntary. Funding for the program would be small-scale: $300 million per year. Moreover, this small investment today could result in potentially great savings in the future by reducing dependence on welfare and other social services.

Typically, marriage promotion programs would provide information about the long-term value of marriage to at-risk high school students. They would teach relationship skills to unmarried couples before the woman became pregnant, with a focus on preventing pregnancy before a couple has made a commitment to healthy marriage.

Marriage programs would also provide marriage and relationship education to unmarried couples at the "magic moment" of a child's birth, and offer marriage-skills training to low-income married couples to improve marriage quality and reduce the likelihood of divorce.

The primary focus of marriage programs would be preventative--not reparative. The programs would seek to prevent the isolation and poverty of welfare mothers by intervening at an early point before a pattern of broken relationships and welfare dependence had emerged. By fostering better life decisions and stronger relationship skills, marriage programs can increase child well-being and adult happiness, and reduce child poverty and welfare dependence (31).

## The Importance of Marriage

Today, nearly one-third of all American children are born outside marriage. That's one out-of-wedlock birth every 35 seconds. Of those born inside marriage, a great many children will experience their parents' divorce before they reach age 18. More than half of the children in the United States will spend all or part of their childhood in never-formed or broken families.

The collapse of marriage is the principal cause of child poverty in the United States. Children raised by never-married mothers are seven times more likely to live in poverty than children raised by their biological parents in intact marriages. Overall, approximately 80 percent of long-term child poverty in the United States occurs among children from broken or never-formed families.

It is often argued that strengthening marriage would have little impact on child poverty because absent fathers earn too little. This is not true. The typical non-married father earns $17,500 per year at the time his child is born. It has been estimated that about 70 percent of poor single mothers would be lifted out of poverty if they were married to their children's father.

This is illustrated in Chart 1, which uses data from the Princeton Fragile Families and Child Well-being Survey, a well-known survey of couples who are unmarried at the time of a child's birth. If the mothers remain single and do not marry the fathers of their children, some 55 percent will be poor. However, if the mothers married the fathers, the poverty rate would drop to 17 percent. (This analysis is based on the fathers' actual earnings in the year before the child's birth.)

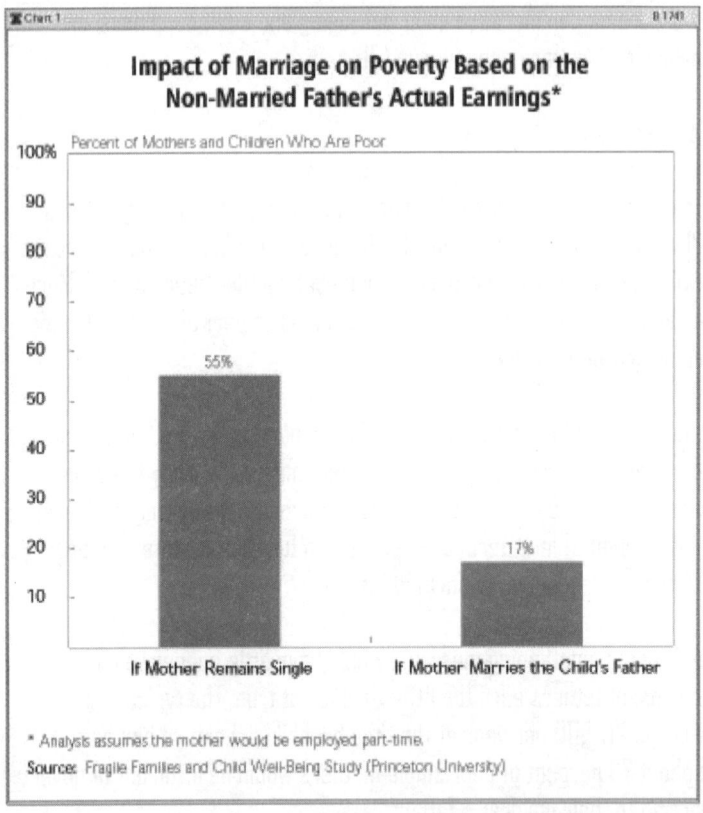

The growth of single-parent families has had an enormous impact on government. The welfare system for children is overwhelmingly a subsidy system for single-parent families. Some three-quarters of the aid to children given through programs such as food stamps, Medicaid, public housing, Temporary Assistance to Needy Families (TANF), and the Earned Income Tax Credit--goes to single-parent families. (See Chart 2.) Each year, government spends over $150 billion in means-tested welfare aid for single parents.

Growing up without a father in the home has harmful long-term effects on children. Compared with similar children from intact families, children raised in single-parent homes are more likely to become involved in crime, to have emotional and behavioral problems, to fail in school, to abuse drugs, and to end up on welfare as adults.

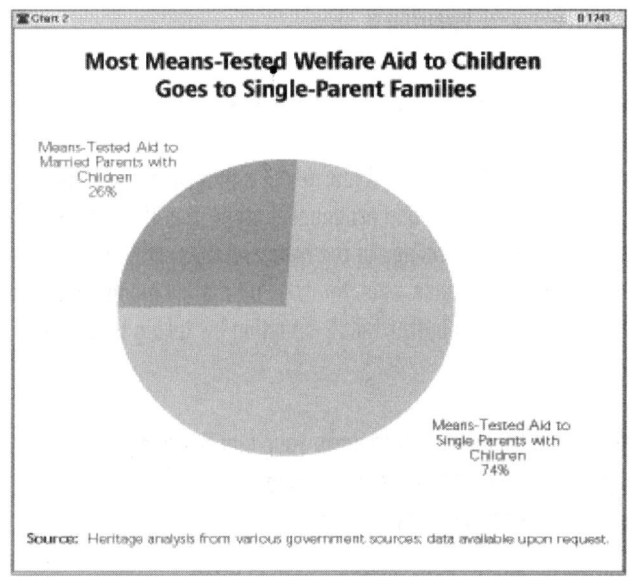

## The Growing Consensus on Promoting Healthy Marriage

The overwhelming evidence of the positive benefits of marriage for children, women, and men has led to a large and growing consensus that government policy should strengthen marriage, not undermine it.

Will Marshall, of the Progressive Policy Institute, and Isabel Sawhill, widely respected welfare and family expert at the Brookings Institution, recently issued a paper entitled "Progressive Family Policy for the 21st Century." Marshall and Sawhill repudiate "the relativist myth that `alternative family forms' were the equal of two-parent families," citing a growing body of evidence showing that, in aggregate, children do best in married, two-parent families. They argue, "A progressive family policy should encourage and reinforce married, two-parent families because they are best for children."

I fully agree with the promotion of healthy marriage in all societies. Unfortunately, this great idea has remained elusive because of the incidence of family violence.

# CHAPTER 9

## How To Strengthen Family Relationships

The ancient Chinese philosopher Lao Tzu said, "A journey of a thousand miles must begin with a single step." It is not how fast one proceeds. Rather, it is the success of the journey that matters. Consider the analogy of the hare and the turtle in a race. Also, remember that through perseverance, even the snail ultimately made it into the Ark. One can begin his/her journey to a better family situation by, taking these initial steps.

- Decide to make a special effort to make your family stronger.
- Learn about family life, marriage, and parenting.
- Keep your priorities and values in mind.

Most people value their families, although many of them are not aware of the importance of improving their family life. It takes hard work to make a successful family. The work put into making a family stronger, however, can be well worth the effort.

I am convinced that people throughout the world must strengthen marriages and family relationships. As previously stated in this book, strong marriages, based on the Divine Blueprint for marriage is a vital component to building strong families and raising healthy, happy, well-educated children.

Fighting together against the forces that undermine family values, and creating a national culture that nurtures and encourages marriage and good family life, must be at the heart of this great nation's public policy. A strong family is a caring family. This includes but is not limited to a nuclear family, stepfamily, single-parent family, or an empty-nest family. All families need periodic nurturing and strengthening of the family relationship.

The Advocates for Youth organization has provided the following suggestions for improving and strengthening relationships (3).

There are at least five "L's" which contribute to strong family relationships.

- Learning. Families are where we learn values, skills, and behavior. Strong families manage and control their learning experiences. They select appropriate television programs. They guide their children into the world outside the home. They do not let social forces rule their family life. They involve themselves in neighborhood, school, government, church, and business in ways that support their family values. Strong families teach by example and learn through experience as they explain and execute their values.
- Loyalty. Strong families learn a sense of give and take in the family, which helps prepare them for the necessary negotiations in other relationships.
- Love. Families share activities and express a great deal of gratitude for one another. Love takes time, affection, and a positive attitude.
- Laughter. Laughing together builds up a family. Laughing at each other divides a family. Families that learn to use laughter in a positive way can release tensions, gain a clearer view, and bond relationships.
- Leadership. Family members, usually the adults, must assume responsibility for leading the family. If no one accepts this vital role, the family will weaken. Each family needs its own special set of rules and guidelines. These rules are based on the family members' greatest understanding of one another. The guidelines pass along from the adults to the children by example, with firmness and fairness.

## Life Patterns of Strong Families

In studies conducted in the United States and around the world, several characteristics of strong families surfaced. These qualities are:

Commitment. Members of strong families are devoted to the well-being and happiness of the other members. They value family unity. Commitment serves as a firm foundation for strong family relationships. This means that:

- The family comes first

- Work responsibilities come second
- Each family member is precious
- Bad times do not destroy relationships
- There is sexual faithfulness to the marriage partner
- Forgiveness is readily available
- Priorities must be established
- Some sacrifices must be made
- Some common goals must be shared
- Traditions are established and cherished
- Love is unconditional

Appreciation. Members of strong families show and talk about their appreciation for one another. Appreciation helps motivate all members to continue to behave positively toward one another. Appreciation in families means:

- Looking for the positive instead of the negative
- Treating family members like our best friends
- Showing love in small ways every day
- Expressing lots of appropriate affection
- Saying, "I love you" a lot
- Praising the accomplishments and strengths of family members
- Gracefully receiving compliments as well as sincerely giving them
- Creating a positive environment in the home
- Remembering (even if you need a list) and celebrating birthdays anniversaries, and special occasions

Communication. Members of strong families work at developing good communication skills and spend a lot of time talking with one another other.

Effective communication means:

- Being open and honest, yet kind
- Listening carefully without distraction
- Checking the meaning of messages, which are not clear?

- Avoiding "mind-reading"
- "Walking a mile" in the other person's shoes
- Trusting one another
- Avoiding criticizing, evaluating, and acting superior
- Dealing with one issue at a time
- Dealing with specifics rather than generalities
- Attacking the problem, not each other
- Having an understanding attitude

Time together. Family time spent together. This:

- Helps eliminate isolation, loneliness, and alienation.
- Helps the family develop an identity—a group unity and a sense of its place in history.
- Helps avoid the "fizzle and die" of some marriage relationships.
- Enhances the communication process.
- Allows opportunity to build on other family strengths.

What exactly are families to do when they are together? The answer is just about anything. They can share:

- Mealtimes
- House and yard chores
- Picnics
- Camping
- Outdoor sports
- Walking or hiking
- Indoor recreation, such as jigsaw puzzles, table games, or a favorite video
- Bowling or going to the movies
- Religious services
- Scouting or 4-H Club activities
- School activities

- Special events like holidays and birthdays

Spiritual wellness. The spiritual dimension in families provides many possible benefits. Spirituality:

- Helps family members maintain a positive outlook on life.
- Provides guidelines for living.
- Provides a sense of freedom and peace.
- Offers support from people who share in a belief system.
- Provides meaningful tradition and ritual.
- Provides a spiritual heritage.
- Provides an expression of character in everyday living.
- Gives an awareness of a divine presence in life.
- Helps families cope during times of trouble.
- Encourages a sense of awe and reverence for life itself.

Coping ability. A variety of coping strategies has been found in strong families, including the following:

- The ability to find something positive in any situation and to focus on that positive element
- Family members unite and pull together when things get tough.
- Strong families get outside help when needed.

Flexibility is another important strategy that strong families use to help get through crises. Strong families bend, change, and adapt; and when the storm is over, they are still intact.

## Chapter 10

## Revelation of the Victorious Vision

In the beginning, man was One with God. God breathed the breathe of life into his nostrils, and he became a living soul. That does not only mean he possessed life. Man was full of the knowledge of God. At that time, his relationship with God was 'good.' Eventually, sin brought about a disconnection between God and humankind.

We fell from grace to grass by allowing the enemy to usurp our birthright. Sin opened the flood gates of hell on earth. Since then, humankind has been trying to reach out to his Creator, to regain the knowledge we lost about Him one more time, so His will 'be done on earth as it is in heaven.' Humankind has been trying to accomplish that in many ways despite the advent of prophets and judges.

Because of His loving kindness, righteousness, and judgment, He sent His Son, Yahshua to die for our sins. On the third day, He raised Him from the dead. By Faith, we will have eternal life in Him.

I do not wish to downplay any religion. I have the utmost respect for all the prophets and religious leaders. I consider myself a modern-day prophet. God speaks to me directly in my dreams, just as he did to certain prophets long, long ago. As stated earlier, the message of this book, I believe, was inspired by God for the benefit of humankind.

Despite the price Yahshua paid on the cross, most people are still not getting the true message. Others continue to drink 'milk' instead of eating 'strong meat' regarding the oracles of God. The time has now come when we must wake up from our spiritual slumber. We must step out in faith and begin feeding ourselves 'strong meat.'

History teaches us that a lot of battles have been fought on earth that are deeply rooted in misguided interpretations of religious principles. We must realize that we are all God's children.

There should be no reason why the lives of many innocent missionaries should be cut short in the crossfire of senseless wars based on misguided religious beliefs.

Also, many people will have to answer the call to help make ONE PLUS ONE EQUALS ONE a success. They might get started off on the right footing. But later they would forget the true meaning of their calling, forget the source of their strength, and become egoistic, greedy, or think they have done it all by themselves. When that happens, they will be replaced and others will be found to carry on the work ahead. It requires faith and obedience to make this vision a reality.

God does not choose people who have the ability to accomplish a task like this based on their own ability, knowledge, power or foresight. Or else, they would get the glory. Remember, He is a "jealous God".

He chooses people based on their FAITH and gives them the ability, vision, and all the tools they need to accomplish His purpose under the ANOINTING of the HOLY SPIRIT. Presented in the following section and in subsequent chapters are the victorious visions for victory given to me by God for $21^{st}$ Century families:

1. Victorious $21^{st}$ Century Families Must Get Back One with God

I consider ONE PLUS ONE EQUALS ONE an inspired book of vision for all families worldwide. Let me caution the reader that some of the subject material presented in this section might not sound 'politically correct.' However, I have come to discover that people usually appreciate the *TRUTH*.

The Bible teaches that "ye shall know the Truth, and the Truth shall make you free." Therefore, I will push personal feelings aside and do what I believe God has asked me to do without fear or favor.

The first and foremost vision for victorious 21st Century families is to get back one with God. Cultivation of this relationship with Him entails:

Obedience, Belief, Trusting, Hearing, Speaking, Praising, and having FAITH in His Word (1, 2).

These seven (I) elements will revive the Holy Spirit that would reveal and lead us into all truth. Then and only then shall we be truly free to love our neighbors as ourselves. Then and only then will we be empowered to see the Light that will lead us through the Narrow gate so we can acquire the tools necessary to salvage our marriages and strengthen our family relationships.

The reason God created humankind was to bless us. God has not changed His position on that matter. He came that we might have life and have it more abundantly. As we embark on ONE PLUS ONE EQUALS ONE, we will run into several roadblocks set up strategically by the devil to frustrate our efforts. But we must not allow him to succeed. He is a liar and the father of lies.

God still wants us to have life and have it more abundantly. He is Yahuah (Jehovah) God. He changes not. He still loves us, has invested, and continues to invest in us. When Yashua's disciples asked Him to teach them how to pray, one of the things He asked them to request was, "Thy will be done on earth as it is in heaven." The devil does not live in heaven, neither will God create a heaven on earth for the devil. His rightful place is in the bottomless pit!

We have been without the abundant life in our marriage and family relationships for too long. We must believe that this is the millennium when change for the better will come for all families globally. We must work at it within the blueprint of divine marriage. Unfortunately, the evil one is determined to put "storms" in our lives to make us miserable; thereby, contradicting God's intentions for us.

The storms he would send our way may come in various forms. They might show up as financial distress or marital difficulties. They might show up as problems in our communications or relationships. At other times, they might show up in the form of sickness or disease.

The devil is a formidable adversary. Yet, his military strategies have always been the same. He works to attack our bodies, mind, will, and heart. He sometimes varies his strategy, and might manifest his lies in the form of depression, anger, jealousy, or stress. He could show up in the form of work-related issues or through a whole array of schemes. Nevertheless, we must not let him mislead or discourage us. We owe it to ourselves, and our families to be victorious. we can have a successful and prosperous family. we can have a happy marriage.

We have already won the victory through Yahshua (Jesus) who strengthens us. Let us stand our ground. Resist the devil, and he will flee from us by the power in the name of the Anointed One. We must be firm. we cannot give up. Stand on the promises of God.

Job 14: 1 states that, "man that is born of a woman is of few days, and full of trouble." That is to say, Satan is always going to and fro on the earth seeking whom he may devour or resist (Job 1: 6-11; 2: 1-6, Zechariah 3: 1-7).

The unfortunate thing about this is that many families of the world do not get the opportunity to participate in the accusations the enemy levels against them in the spirit realm. They are physical beings. The devil is a spirit. What they see are the physical manifestations of the wars that occur in the spiritual realm.

Some people might be aware of the actions of the enemy but choose not to believe in the existence of 'evil spirits or its ability to impact their lives.

From a spiritual standpoint, I have often wondered why God might have allowed the pain and suffering we have experienced, and continue to suffer through that which have come upon us. Could it be that He wanted us to go through all those changes for His Son? Could it be that He wanted to teach us some valuable lesson such as humility, make us stronger, teach us patience, or better prepare us to console others who face the storms of life?

While any or all of the foregoing might be reasonable options, we must be aware that our actions sometimes open the door for the devil impact our lives negatively (Deuteronomy 18: 10-11).

We must remember that God is not the architect of confusion or deception. Therefore, we should be able to distinguish between God's voice, and that of the devil's (Deuteronomy 10: 22)

We know that God's voice liberates us from sin and oppression. He brings us assurances of joy, peace, love, patience, etc., or what we commonly refer to as "the fruit of the spirit." In contrast, the devil's voice deceives, contradicts God's word, and leads us into sin. We must know who we are, and more importantly, whose we are. We must not forget the limitless power given us in the name of Yahshua (Jesus). Similarly, we must know how to tap into that power, and stand on the promises of God. To do that we must continually strive to exemplify characteristics of the Children of Light. We have both the power and authority to resist the devil, and claim happy and strong family relationships.

One thing I know is that, no matter what predicaments we face in our marriage or family relations, if we look up to Him for deliverance, he will provide a way of escape for us. These avenues of escape might be miraculous. He might cause us to go into hiding to escape danger or possibly death.

He might take us away to glory or he might give us the ability to cope with our circumstance. He might choose to give us boldness, personal conviction or courage, or he might decide to be with us in the "Fire of Affliction."

Remember Shadrach, Meshach, and Abednego in the Book of Daniel? God was with them in the fiery furnace. The scriptures stated that when they came out, the fire had no 'power' over their bodies, that their hair was not 'singed,' their coats did not 'change', nor the 'smell of fire had passed on them.' The fires of family violence, miscommunication, divorce, or financial distress have no power over us. We can have a happy marriage and strong family relationship.

Begin to obey, believe, trust, worship, hear, speak, and have unwavering faith in the Word of God. These activities enable us to walk in the Light, and make us "spiritually sensitive."

The Psalmist accurately stated this as, "In lumine tuo videbimus lumen" ( "In your Light we shall see Light.")

While a student, I once visited a poor family. I got up in the middle of the night to get a drink of water from the kitchen. When I flicked on the light, I saw numerous roaches running in various directions.

At another time, I took my children to Carlsbad Caverns in New Mexico when they were quite young. At one point, the tour guide turned off the artificial lights in the cavern to demonstrate the total darkness in almost 1,100 feet below the surface of the earth. He lit a candle, that shined brightly amidst the darkness at that depth.

Those two experiences taught me that the greatest impact of light was in darkness. That was why Yahshua (Jesus) encouraged us to let our light shine before men so that they would see our good works and glorify the Father in heaven. That was why Yahshua came into this world at night. That was why humankind was placed on earth at night.

That was also why the greatest miracles performed by God, usually took place at night, specifically at midnight. Let me share a few of these with you:

- We know that Yahshua was born at night, probably close to midnight. He hinted that His return might be at the midnight hour (Matthew 25:6).
- It was at the midnight hour that God sent the 10$^{th}$ plague on Egypt. Pharaoh then got the message and opened the way for the Exodus.
- God woke up Samson at midnight. He led him to surprise the unprepared Philistines (Judges 16:3).
- Boaz discovered and protected Ruth at midnight.
- The litigant woman's child was kidnapped at midnight. Later, the child was given back to her by King Solomon's judicial wisdom
- Job was reminded by Elihu that death could come to anyone at midnight.
- According to Psalm 119:62, the psalmist chose the midnight hour for his deepest prayer.
- In Luke 11:5, Yahshua (Jesus) told a parable that depicted that the midnight hour was when the importuning of the breadless neighbor produced a favorable response.
- An earthquake was produced by the midnight prison prayer of Paul and Silas. It flung the prison doors open, and converted the jailer (Acts 16:25).

Similarly, in Troas, it was the midnight hour when Paul's greatest miracle of raising Eutychus from the dead occurred.

When the devil attacks or his schemes linger on in your relationship, you have to know how to fight back. If you have done all you can without much success, don't give up. Remember the midnight hour is the time when the above 'miracles' took place.

Yes, there is something mysterious and special about the midnight hour when it comes to moving the Spirit of God. You might get your breakthrough at this hour. You can rightly say, "I am going to wait till the midnight hour!"

Of course, it is an established fact that Yahshua performed many miracles in daylight. Do not be afraid to stand on the promises of God.

I would like you to know that the living God is a good God. He has given us all the tools we need to defeat the devil. He wants us to have life and have it more abundantly. The key is to stand on His Word through Faith:

- Hebrews 6: 12. "Be not slothful, but follower of them who through faith and patience inherit the Promise."
- 2 Peter 3: 9-10, "the Lord is not slack concerning his promise….shall be burned up."
- 2 Corinthians 1: 20, "For all the promises of God in Him are yea, and in Him Amen, unto the Glory of God by us."

In order to function properly in life, and to enjoy our marriage and family relationship, all human beings need six dimension of well-being to lead a harmonious life. These include: spiritual, physical, social, occupational, intellectual, and emotional well-being. All six must be kept in proper balance to maintain an individual's well-being. The control of these factors and all of our actions originate in the mind.

The mind becomes the natural playground or center for spirituals battles. Remember the old adage, "The devil tempts most men. But idle minds tempt the devil."

Let us look at some examples of God's promises to the believer in the following scriptures:

- Deuteronomy 7: 12-18
- Deuteronomy 8 : 18
- Deuteronomy 9: 3
- Deuteronomy 11: 13-15; 25
- Deuteronomy 28 : 1-14
- I Corinthians 7 : 2-5
- Matthew 28: 18-20. ' all power is given unto me...even unto the end of the world'.
- Mark 3: 15. 'And to have power to heal sicknesses, and to cast out devils.'
- Luke 9: 1. '...and gave them power and authority over all devils, and to cure diseases.'
- Luke 10: 19. '..power to tread on serpents and scorpions...shall harm you.'
- Ephesians 1: 20-23. '...and raised him from the dead...principality power, dominion..that filleth all in all.'
- Colossians 1: 16-17. 'him were all things created...all things consist.'
- Matthew 17: 27. '...and cast an hook...for me and thee.'
- Deuteronomy 8: 18. 'Gives Thee power to get wealth.'

Know that you can stand on the promises of God by exercising faith in the Word through effectual fervent prayer. Here are some additional supporting scriptures filled with encouragement:

- Ephesians 6:16
- James 5: 16
- Matthew 21: 22
- Mark 11: 23-24; 9: 29

- John 14: 12-14
- I Corinthians 7: 5

As you embark on ONE PLUS ONE EQUALS ONE, you must watch, and pray unceasingly. I know prayer works. Prayer will get your marriage back on track, and your family relationship on solid ground. Let me provide you a few supporting verses of scripture that clearly confirm the power of prayer:

- Joshua 10: 12-14          Prayer of Joshua
- Nehemiah 1: 5-11; 2: 8    Prayer of Nehemiah
- Daniel 9: 19-22           Prayer of Daniel
- I Samuel 30:6, 18-19      Prayer of David
- I Chronicles 4: 10        Prayer of Jabez
- Matthew 26:39             Prayer of Yahshua (Jesus)
- I Corinthians 7: 2

Be assured of your victory in Yahshua, who will never fail you.

## Proper equipment for Spiritual Warfare

Many people who have been called to embark on the vision to victory in ONE PLUS ONE EQUALS ONE must not be ill-equipped for the work. It is your responsibility to put on or learn how to put on the full armor of God.

The Bible teaches that the weapons of our warfare are not carnal. No one goes to war without assessing what he/she needs to win the war. God has given us in the Bible what we need to win spiritual battles. The same equipment will work for whatever difficulties we might be facing in our marriage or family relationship.

We are bound to face struggles with the enemy. In this regard, we must be properly educated in 'spiritual warfare' to be knowledgeable on how to resist the enemy. I have already covered how certain spirits can derail marriage and family relationships.

A lot of people 'chicken out' in doing battle with the enemy because they feel God had not called the believer to undertake such battles. The fact of the matter is that the devil does not care what our understanding of the Bible is. If he perceives you as a threat, he will engage you (seeking whom he may destroy) even though all you want to do is go about God's business and not engage the devil.

You see, the devil is a spirit and sees in the spirit realm. He sees God's blessings coming to you and does whatever he can to block it whether or not you have stepped on his toes. What did Job do to the devil to deserve what he got? On the other hand, what did Joshua the high priest do to the devil for the devil to resist him?

Some of us are bound to have additional problems in our personal lives such as conflict in relationships, financial pressures, time demands, illness, personality conflicts, job loss, or even death. In these and other situations, we are to draw nearer to God and wait for Him. However, the enemy would have us do just the opposite - to complain and run away from God.

By waiting upon the Lord, He will renew our strength so we will mount up with wings as eagles, so we will run and not be weary, and so we will walk and not faint. (Isaiah 40:31).

## Why Must We Wait Upon GOD?

- Because of whom God is, and what He has proven to be very capable of doing throughout history. We must know the God in whom we have placed your Faith. He also will do what He said He would do. It may not be according to your calendar. He has His own calendar, that is why we must learn to wait upon Him.

- Because of who we are and our limitations. Remember, God will not do for you what you can do for yourself. He steps in where your abilities and capabilities end.

- To sustain and satisfy.

- To strengthen and enable.

- To build character.

- To lift His children out of despair and cause them to praise Him.

- To encourage others and provide a forum to witness.

You see, an eagle uses storms for his benefit. He carefully discerns the strong wind patterns and gains their advantage so he actually soars to greater heights.

We need to learn from the eagle's example. We need to use trials and tribulations to our advantage. We need to recognize where the storms are coming from and why they are occurring so we can soar over them and achieve patience and spiritual growth.

We do not always follow Galatians 5:16 as a guideline, which tells us to walk in the Spirit. As a result, the lusts of the flesh (greed, selfishness, lust, pride, etc.) often take over because of our inherited sinful nature.

However, Romans 13:12 tells us to put on our spiritual "armor of light" so that we can stand up to the onslaught of these powerful adversaries which try to influence us. We must resist principalities on the turf God has given us, by walking in the Spirit on the spiritual level, with weapons appropriate to the conflict (8).

God has called His children to liberty. Hold our ground. God does not ask you and me to invade any territory for Him or march into new grounds. The ground is ours; all we have to do is stand fast and hold it. We should not let the enemy intimidate us or steal from usu. Yahshua gained the victory, and all we have to do is maintain it.

Below is a summary of each of the seven armaments for our spiritual warfare:

## Sword of the Spirit

The Sword of the Spirit is the Word of God. By speaking and praying the Word of God, be assured us will breakdown strongholds in the spiritual realm. There could be hindrances to our prayers for various reasons. We must be careful to ensure we have met the proper requirements for our prayers to be answered. Our prayers might be hindered for any or all of the following reasons, according to the scriptures:

- Failure to emulate appropriate qualities as children of God.

- Lack of Faith in Him.

- Not demanding. We have not because we have not demanded in His name.

- Praying with the wrong motives.

- Praying outside the will of God.

- Holding on to the spirit of unforgiveness.

- Not resisting the enemy. When we resist the enemy in Yahshua's name. He has no choice but to flee from us!

- Not giving Him the praise.

- Praying to other gods.

- Not waiting patiently for Him.

- Refusing to do our part.

- Stinginess. It is more blessed to give than to receive.

- Repetition of vain words.

- Assuming God is obligated to us.

- Family relation trouble.

- Not praying specifically in the name of Yahshua (Jesus).

Yahshua the living Word defeated Satan at Calvary. Similarly, the spoken word now enforces that victory. As a believer, the Word has given us authority.

## Prayer and Supplication

II Corinthians 10:4 teaches that prayer and supplication break down strongholds in the heavens.

## Helmet of Salvation

The mind is the battleground for spiritual warfare (1,2). The helmet of salvation guards our minds, for the battle against the enemy in the mind. The helmet of salvation assures us of two things:

a. We will have eternal life in heaven.
b. God has a special plan for us.

## Shield of Faith

Faith casts out fear. God has not given us the spirit of fear. If you want to live a fearless life, we must read, study, and meditate on the Word of God.

## Breastplate of Righteousness

Although our "righteousness is of filthy rags" according to Isaiah 64:6, we are justified and made righteous in God's eyes because of our faith in His Son – Yahshua (Habakkuk 2:4)

## Belt of Truth

We need to "provide for honest things not only in the sight of the Lord, but also in the sight of men." (II Corinthians 8:21). We must be truthful in all things. When trials and tribulations come our way, we must stand on the promises of God.

## Sandals of Peace

According to II Timothy 4:2, and Mark 16:15, we must preach the Word and carry it to every creature.

## Maintain a focus on our Objectives

Joshua had favor with God because he was focused and obedient in all the commands and assignments he was given.

Despite all the odds that stood in His way, Yahshua maintained His focus on accomplishing God's purpose for man all the way until the end.

## How Victorious 21$^{st}$ Century Families Can Tap into God's Blessings

The blessings for our marriages and family relationships I am talking about in ONE PLUS ONE EQUALS ONE are ours for the asking. They are ours to keep. However, we must know how to tap in to them because the blessings are limitless. We cannot place a value on them.

Yahshua (Jesus) taught us that the Father dwells in Him, and He dwells in the Father. Thus, He and the Father are One. He also assured us that if we abide in Him, He would abide in us. That means, He would give us the right to be called the sons and daughters of God. Finally, He stated unequivocally, that all that the Father has are His. Logically, we can state, that if we faithfully abide in Him, then we can earn the right to have access to all that the Father has.

I read somewhere that Bill Gates has about 27 billion dollars in his foundation. Now, if Bill Gates, or the heirs to the Wal-Mart fortune gave you a blank check and asked you to write and cash any amount you desired to take care of your physical needs, would you write a check for $700 or $700 million to undertake a project of interest to you that would make a difference in your life or in the life of others?

Would people in their rightful mind go about life in pain and suffering in a miserable marriage or family relationship that is in shambles when their Father, who loves them to the point that He gave His only begotten Son to lay down His life for their salvation has given them total access to unlimited power, wealth, peace, joy, and happiness? Of course not!

It might be that one does not know how to tap into God's wealth. Let me share with you plainly how to tap into God's unlimited wealth, wealth that cannot be destroyed by rust or moth.

Actually, God has given us a blank check signed and sealed in the name of Yahshua for all His children. Let us look at some scriptures that support this assertion:

- *Mark 11: 23-24 states,* " For verily I say unto you that whosoever shall say unto this mountain, Be thou cast into the sea; and shall not doubt in his heart; but shall believe that those things which he saith shall come to pass; he shall have whatsoever he saith.

    Therefore I say unto you what things soever ye desire, when ye pray, believe that ye receive them, and ye shall have them."

- *John 14: 12-14 states,* "Verily, verily I say unto you, he that believeth in me, the works that I do shall he do also; and greater works than these shall he do; because I go unto my Father.

    In addition, whatsoever ye shall ask in my name, that will I do, that the Father may be glorified in the Son.

    If ye shall ask anything in my name, I will do it."
    That includes a happy marriage and strong family relationship.

- Genesis 12: 2          He will bless and make us a great nation.
- Genesis 12: 3          He will bless those that bless us
- Genesis 26: 3          He will be with us and bless us
- Psalm 28: 9            He will bless our inheritance
- Deut. 15: 10; 16: 15   He will bless us in all our

|  |  |
|---|---|
|  | works, and our increase |
| - Psalm 115: 13. | Bless us if we fear Him |
| - Genesis 1; 22 | Bless us to be fruitful and multiply |
| - Deut. 7: 4 | We shall be blessed above all people |
| - Deut. 28: 3-6 | We shall be blessed in the city, field, fruit of our bodies, basket, when we go out or come in |
| - Jon 42; 12 | He will bless our older years with life and health |
| - Psalm 41: 1 | He will bless us if we consider the poor |
| - Psalm 84: 12 | Bless us if we trust in Him |
| - Mark 8: 7 | Bless what we turn over to Him |
| - John 20: 29 | Bless us if we have faith in Him |
| - Acts 20: 35 | Bless us if we give rather than receive from others |
| - Romans 4; 7; 18 | Bless us by forgiving our iniquities |
| - Romans 4: 18 | Bless us by not imputing our sins |
| - Proverbs 10: 22 | Bless us and make us rich |
| - Ephesians 1; 3 | Bless us in heavenly places |
| - Nehemiah 13: 2 | Turn the curse into a blessing |

'Blessing' can be defined as "the gift of divine favor." Better yet, biblical scholars define it as "the act of declaring or wishing favor and goodness upon others." Blessing is not only the good effect of words; it also has the power to bring the words to pass.

In the Bible, important persons blessed those with less power or influence. For example, the patriarchs pronounced blessings on their children, often near their own deaths (Genesis 49: 1-28).

The act of blessing is so powerful that even if spoken by mistake, once it is given, it could not be taken back (Genesis 27: 33).

Leaders often blessed people, especially when getting ready to leave them. Examples of these included Moses (Deut. 33); Joshua (Joshua 22: 6-7), and Yahshua (Luke 24: 50).

Equals could also bless each other by being friendly (Genesis 12: 3). One could also bless God by showing gratitude to Him (Deut. 8: 10) or in songs of praise (Psalm 103: 1-2).

The opposite of blessing is cursing (Deut. 27: 11-26). There is a tendency for certain people to 'put a curse' on others for various reasons. That is not a good thing to do. Note that Proverbs 25: 22 encourages us that if we do well to those who wish us evil, we "heap coals of fire upon their head, and the Lord shall reward thee." This is a hard thing to do because the natural reaction to a curse is to curse back.

Initiated or ordained persons must especially be careful what they say and what they do, even in private. What many people do not know is that when the people of a religion appoint individuals from among themselves to have access to the reservoir of grace, those chosen individuals receive a formal initiation or ordination.

It is believed that Christian ministers, for example, have "sacerdotal angels" (priestly) who assist them in the functions of their office. Therefore, one must be very careful what he/she says about chosen religious leaders. It can bring a curse unto him or her.

For this reason the Bible instructs us to bless; that is, ask for the person's benefit (Matthew 5: 44; Luke 6: 28; Romans 12: 14). Subsequently, God will take care of the rest, and we would be held blameless for any consequences that arise upon those who try to do us harm.

The word 'blessing' comes from the Hebrew word "baruch" (15) which means "Camel". It is also the name of three or four men in the Old Testament, as follows:

- A son of Zabbai, Baruch who helped Nehemiah repair the walls of Jerusalem (Nehemiah 3: 20; 10: 6)
- A son of Col-Hozeh, who returned captive of the tribe of Judah (Nehemiah 11: 5)
- The scribe or secretary of Jeremiah (Jeremiah 32: 12-16; 36: 1-32; 45: 1-5)

Camels were indispensable for traveling the desert routes, carrying heavy weights or loads on their backs.

Nevertheless, before the camel can receive a load of 'goodies,' he must first kneel down on his leathery knees and then get up. Sometimes, while it is traveling through the rough, rugged desert routes, some of the load is shifted out of place, and its owner must stop its movement, and straighten it up.

Finally, when the camel gets to its destination, tired, and weary, it must kneel down once again in order for the load to be removed off its back so it could feel light once again or be made whole.

I wonder if there is a family reading ONE PLUS ONE EQUALS ONE at this very moment that needs a blessing right now. Know that God is the source of all blessings. He is our Master, Savior, and the Father of Lights above. Like the camel, we must kneel down right now in His presence and ask Him to load us up with the blessings He has specifically for our family and us.

But because the troubles of the world can sometimes be rugged, sharp, or a little too hot to handle by ourselves, we need to learn how to stand on God's promises by believing, trusting, obeying, hearing, speaking, worshipping, and having faith in His Word so that He will give us tough feet and the spiritual leathery knees. Like the Camel, we need to kneel down and receive His blessings for our family.

Otherwise, the fiery darts of the enemy would cause us to move from our positions, with our filthy clothes still on, thus preventing us from receiving our new clothes and assured blessings from God.

I wonder if there's a family reading ONE PLUS ONE EQUALS ONE right now whose blessings from God or healing of his or her family relationship have shifted out of place and who needs to tell his or her soul to be "still for the Lord is on your side" to straighten up the load he/she is carrying.

I urge you to stand still and see the salvation of the Lord; say to your soul, "whatever my lot, thou has taught me to say it is well with my soul." Say to your soul that 'those that wait upon the Lord shall renew their strength; they shall mount up with wings like eagles, they shall run and not be weary, they shall walk and not faint." Yes, assure your soul of the following:

- Is 37: 34, " By the way that he came, by the same shall he returns."
- Is. 41: 10, "Fear thou not for I am with thee, be not dismayed for I am your God; I will strengthen thee, yea, I will help thee; Yea, I will uphold thee with the right hand of my righteousness"
- Is. 54: 17, " No weapon that is formed against thee shall prosper."
- Is. 65: 24, " And it shall come to pass, that before they call, I will answer; and while they are yet speaking, I will hear."

I wonder if there is another family reading ONE PLUS ONE EQUALS ONE right now who is almost at the end of their long journey of waiting for God's blessings for his or her family, but who has grown tired and weary of waiting.

I submit to you that you need to go down on your knees right now before the throne of Grace and ask the Good Master to take away or lighten our burden so we can be made whole in faith once again to receive our blessings for a return journey of happiness, joy, peace, and the success we once knew.

The Bible gives several examples of God's blessings to people. These blessings include giving life, riches, fruitfulness, or plenty (Genesis 1: 22, 28). His greatest blessing is turning man away from evil (Acts 3: 25-26) and forgiving our sins (Romans 4: 7-8).

# God's Guarantees of Security & Protection for Victorious 21$^{st}$ Century Families

I have heard great preachers teach on the Anointing. Among other things, the Anointing gives the believer supernatural authority, ability, attractiveness, access to preferred places, and divine protection. Another frequently quoted scripture that gives a lot of security to families of the world is Isaiah 54: 17 which reads, "No weapon that is formed against thee shall prosper, and every tongue that shall rise against thee in judgment thou shall condemn (declare guilty).

Yet, I have seen repeatedly different bad things happening to families of the world. Some get abused, cheated, mistreated, or even oppressed by forces of darkness. Several explanations are usually given for the believer's demise, namely, God might have allowed it to teach the believer a lesson or prepare him or her for something better. It might also be that we have contradicted God's law, and He is out to punish us. However, let us look again at the second scripture cited above.

It clearly does not state that "no weapons shall be formed against us" It is evident that weapons would be formed against us. However, if such weapons were formed without the consent of God, they would fail. One thing we know for sure is that God makes no mistakes, cannot lie, and is the ultimate and Supreme Creator of the Universe.

Yahshua (Jesus) also assured us that "He would not leave us or forsake us," and that we could "ask anything in my name, and I will do it." That includes divine protection.

As we embark on this new vision for victorious 21$^{st}$ century families in ONE PLUS ONE EQUALS ONE, let us not forget that the road ahead might not always be easy. What, then, must all families of the world do to remain in God's assurance of protection?

Before we get into that, let us examine the types of protection rendered by God. Genesis 15:1, the I AM God states, "I am thy shield, and exceeding great reward." That means God is ready, willing, and able to protect the believer and his or her property and wealth if the believer places his or her Trust in Him rather than in man.

In order to be assured of victory in ONE PLUS ONE EQUALS ONE we must always put God primarily in one's decision-making process, learn to wait for Him, and most of all Trust in his truthfulness and ability to do what is best for us.

Unfortunately, some people take steps in advance of God's prompting, not knowing how to hear the voice of God. They follow the lead of man or themselves, thereby placing them outside the will of God and setting themselves up for trouble.

Satan always tries to tempt us. He gets us preoccupied with material things, while people around us are perishing. In the Old Testament, Abram declared he would not take any rewards from the King of Sodom. Because of that refusal, Jehovah said to him, "Do not be afraid, Abram. I am your shield, your exceeding great reward," thus making him both protected and very wealthy.

In II Samuel 22:3, 36, Psalm 18:35; and Psalm 3:3, it is clearly stated that God is our shield of our salvation from the enemy. Plainly summarized, that means "He is my shield, and the horn of my salvation."

God completely and unequivocally protected David from all his enemies. All his enemies including Saul died; the kingdom was unified under his leadership, and Israel's foes were beaten back. Refer to David's Song (vs. 2-51).

How did David secure God's shield of protection? His spiritual secrets were as follows. David:

- Trusted in God (vs. 3)
- Praised and worshiped God even under difficult circumstances (vs.4)
- Obeyed His WORD (vs. 22)
- Had faith in the WORD (vs. 30)
- Thanked and spoke the WORD (vs. 50)
- Believed in the WORD (vs.29)
- Heard the WORD (vs.7)

The word *trust* meant he relied on or on the *Truth* of God.

In Psalms 28: 7; Psalm 33: 20-22, we are assured that the Lord is our strength and shield. God assures us of His help, and protection from the enemy if we Trust in Him.

For example, whenever all families of the world tried to do something for their own good, their activities were often thwarted by fear that others instilled in them.

The psalmist and his people trusted in Jehovah as their helper and protector. They found true happiness by putting all their confidence in His Holy name. All they ask is that they might continue to bask in the sunshine of His steadfast love as they continue to depend on Him alone. If that worked for the psalmist, we can expect the same as we embark on ONE PLUS ONE EQUALS ONE. God is no respecter of persons.

In Psalm 35: 1-3, and again in Proverbs 30:5, we are assured that God can protect us from friends-turned-traitors, such that their devilish plots might be foiled and repulsed. David called on God to arm himself with a generous supply of weapons and thereby to deal summarily with those professed friends who turned out to be his cruel adversaries.

David wanted God to reach over for His shield and buckler and move into action, hurling His well-aimed spear and then saying to David in an aside, "I'll take care of them, and be your Savior," and for their devilish plots to be foiled and repulsed.

In Psalm 84:11-12, we learned that the Lord God is a sun and shield. The Lord is a 'sun,' providing illumination through the darkness and a 'shield' for protection against the scorching heat along the way.

His truth shall be our shield and buckler. Those who trust in the Lord are sure of His protection. That is, there is safety in the Lord. An application of this principle is given in John 11: 7-10.

Yahshua (Jesus) knew that the Jews could not touch Him until He had finished His work. This is true of every believer. He or she is kept by the power of God through faith in Yahshua. Let us refer to Psalms 91: 4-16; and Psalm 119: 114. These identify eight guarantees of God's security (15).

a. Deliverance from hidden dangers (The snare of the bird trapper)
b. Immunity from fatal disease (Noisome pestilence)
c. Shelter and refuge in the Almighty (Cover thee with His feathers)
d. Protection in the Faithfulness of God. What He has said, He would do. This is the Believer's shield and buckler
   - Freedom from fear from four types of dangers.
   - Enemy attacks under cover of night because the cause is hard to identify.
   - Arrow that flies by day are evil plots and slanders of the Wicked.
   - Pestilence that walks in darkness. Physical disease thrives where it is shielded from the sun's rays and moral evil also breeds in the dark (vs. 6).
   - Destruction that wastes at noonday.

e. Safety even in the midst of massacre (vs. 7-8). Even when there's slaughter on a wholesale basis, the believer is absolutely safe. He or she will be a spectator only, free from the possibility of harm.

f. Insurance against calamity (vs. 9-10)

g. Guarded by angelic escort. God had not told Yahshua (Jesus) to jump down the temple. If He had jumped, He would have acted outside the will of God, and then the promise of protection would not have been valid.

h. Victory over the lion and cobra. Satan is the roaring lion (1 Peter 5:8), and the ancient serpent (Rev. 12: 9).

Ephesians 6:16 teaches that "above all, taking on the shield of Faith." We must take the shield of faith so that when the fiery darts of the enemy come zooming at him, they will hit the shield and fall harmlessly to the ground. Faith means firm confidence in God and His word. No matter what darts the enemy hurls at us. We look up to Him and say, "I will Trust in God."

Victorious 21st Century Families Can Overcome the Spirits of Anger, Anxiety, Fear, Depression, and Sadness & Stress.

Life would be so much better if people would not only read but also follow God's principles. It is not enough to quote Biblical passages unless one actually believes what he/she is quoting, and it comes from within his/her heart.

More often than not, I have seen believers quote the scriptures to display their knowledge and enlightenment of biblical teachings. While these feats might be outwardly impressive, the same people in reality keep watching their back for fear of 'something.' They seem to forget that whenever Yahshua spoke, He did so with authority. He said what He meant, and He meant what He said. That was one reason the evil spirits were so afraid of Him. They knew He was serious with them.

Interestingly, a few people who may not necessarily be believers in the traditional sense, seem to understand the impact of fear on people. A famous prizefighter, Muhammad Ali was able to psyche his opponents into defeat by planting fear in their minds. In fact, he became so good at that that he was able to predict the rounds that he could knock them out. Other athletes have taken on Fearful names to intimidate their opponents. They use names such as "Bone Crusher," "Tiger",' "The Rock," and so on.

We must not waver or be double minded regarding the Promises of God. The Book of James teaches us that such a person cannot expect to receive anything from God. Rather, we must be planted firmly in the Word of God through obedience, belief, trust, faith, worship, hearing and speaking the Word.

Yahshua (Jesus) said he came so that we "might have life and have it more abundantly." That means we can expect to lead a happy and fruitful life in Yahshua who is the 'author and finisher of our faith,' and who is "able to do exceeding abundantly above all that we desire."

The Bible clearly instructs us not to "be given to the spirit of fear;" but in all things we should make our requests known through prayer and supplications.

Furthermore, Yahshua taught us to "be anxious for nothing," and to take one day at a time. That was what He meant when he said, "boast not thyself for tomorrow for thou know not what a day may bring forth." Similarly, He admonished us "not to let the sun go down on our anger."

Yet when we look around us today, we find many people bound, oppressed, and afflicted by the spirits of anger, fear, sadness, depression, anxiety, and stress. People take all kinds of pills to help them sleep or cope with anger, anxiety, depression, or fear.

They invest in all sorts of equipment and services to guarantee their security from fear. Others do all they can to avoid strangers and even neighbors for several reasons including fear. A great deal of illnesses today, however, can be attributed to these spirits, especially the spirit of fear.

Now, why did Yahshua spend time encouraging us not to allow such spirits to overwhelm us? It is because the devil operates through these spirits, especially the spirit of fear. Our minds are the natural battleground for implantation of such spirits.

Sadly, many people we consider "successful" or "anointed" did not and have not grasped the true meaning of those principles. If we study the lives of Saul, David, and the greatest monarch in history Solomon we find out that though wealthy, prominent, and anointed, they led very miserable lives and were usually in fear of "something."

Nicodemus, the Rich Young Ruler, the Prodigal Son, and Yahshua's (Jesus) disciples, James and John, though anointed and in prominent positions all looked for happiness and success. They were also in fear of "something." At one point, Yahshua had to encourage His disciples to "be of good courage, it is I, be not afraid."

In today's mega churches, Pastors and Bishops, no matter how well they preach or teach, have 'bodyguards' with earphones escorting them to and from the pulpits because of the fear of 'something.' Presidents and famous and wealthy people also maintain tight security because of the fear of 'something.'

Scientific studies clearly reveal that those who are subjected to sustained stress die prematurely. Because of the importance of these elements in our spiritual life, I would like to devote time to discuss them. I would also like to recommend that this lesson be shared with the youth of our families because these spirits affect them as well.

As we embark on ONE PLUS ONE EQUALS ONE, it is quite likely that we would encounter those who do not want us to succeed. They might try to instill these spirits in us. However, we must not give in to their whims and caprices.

A few years ago, someone composed a song entitled, "Don't Worry Be Happy." That song won a high award. I wonder then whether that musician knew what "happiness" really was. "Happiness" is difficult to define, and it means many different things to different people.

The word 'happiness' can be defined as a state in which all our emotional chemistry is at its best. In this utopian state, we do not find any cause for alarm. We tend to be healthy to have adequate financial resources, to be happily married to the right person, and to be raising healthy children. It must be noted that true happiness only comes from God. The opposite of happiness is sadness. In a sad state, we might be emotionally distraught. Some people might experience loneliness, might be going through transitions or divorce. Others might feel constantly threatened financially; they might live from paycheck to pay check.

Our state of happiness or sadness affects our emotions. The most obvious emotion we express is fear. This is the reason why Yahshua (Jesus) encouraged us not to be given to the spirit of fear. Fear can be very devastating on our bodies. It could lead to stress and depression which weaken our immune system. It is widely known in the scientific community that people who are subjected to prolonged and consistent stress tend to die prematurely.

Furthermore, fear could be the underlying cause of certain sleep disturbances. We cannot afford to be bound by the spirit of fear! It affects us when we are awake or asleep. However, we can conquer the spirit of fear planted in our marriage or family relationship. Believers in the vision for victorious 21st century families in ONE PLUS ONE EQUALS ONE should strive not to be subjected to the spirit of fear.

The following principles are helpful to overcome the spirit of fear:

- Try not to dwell on a fearful situation too long. Understand that feeling fear and working through it is an inevitable part of life.
- Remember that whatever you are going through is not entirely new to humankind. You might know someone who went through tough times and survived.
- Share your fears with a trustworthy colleague or friend.
- Knowledge is power. Therefore, educate yourself on your particular situation. You will be better able to deal with it then.
- Change your physiology through meditation or by listening to your favorite songs.
- Draw inspiration from others. You should Pray and ask the Holy Spirit for guidance. That is one of His jobs. Take advantage of it.

- Focus on what you get right, not what you get wrong. You might find your successes outweigh your failures.

- Our youth must ask opinions from responsible parents, or guardians or responsible adults, teachers, youth ministers, or counselors for example. They must avoid irresponsible individuals who might use their predicament as a steppingstone to lure them into inappropriate situations or take advantage of them.

Anger which is anathema to the success of ONE PLUS ONE EQUALS ONE comes in various degrees. A combination of anger and hunger can be very dangerous indeed. Anger, if not properly controlled, can lead to difficulties in relationships with others. It can result in acts of aggression and physical violence. It arises from two main factors:

- Physical feelings we experience in the body. It is a state of the mind because all our physical actions originate from the mind.
- The way one perceives a certain situation.

In the angry state, one tends to blame of oneself, others or the system. We must learn to work on "self." Here are some suggestions for managing anger:

- Take responsibility for our actions and decisions. Do not point fingers at others. If we do, we will find three pointing back at us.

- Get away from the situation that is stressing us out. Remember the Book of Proverbs teaches that a soft answer softens wrath.

- If we are aware of something within our power that we can do to change the outcome of the situation, do it. Otherwise, we must accept our lot. Remember life may not always be fair but God is good all the time. We must endeavor to see something good out of the situation in which we find ourselves.

- We should learn to stop blaming ourselves. We all make mistakes. That is part of life. It is only God who cannot make mistakes. Learn from your mistakes and try not to repeat the same mistakes.

Additional evils that might hamper the success of the vision in ONE PLUS ONE EQUALS ONE include depression and stress. I once heard former President Richard Nixon say that, "When the going gets tough, only the tough get going." During difficult times, such as unemployment, stress sets in often resulting in conflicts with spouses, or poor parenting practices that may cause problems for adolescents in school achievement, peer relations, anti-social behavior, self-confidence, depression, and substance abuse.

Many individuals and families fail to recognize the signs of trouble in their homes. Stress can manifest itself in many varied ways. Below are some early warning signs of emotional trouble:

- Anxiety or depression. Severe, intense feelings of anxiety or depression
- Withdrawal or isolation. Withdrawn, alone, lack of friends and support
- Helplessness and hopelessness. Sense of complete powerlessness, a hopeless feeling.

- Alcohol abuse. There's a link between drinking and suicide.
- Previous suicide attempts.
- Suicidal plan. Frequent or constant thoughts with a specific plan in mind.
- Cries for help. Makes a plan for a burial plot, buys large amounts of life insurance, writes will, gives favorite possessions away, and reconciles injured friendships.
- Talks about Suicide. 'I am calling it quits'; 'maybe, my family will be better off without me.'

How To Recognize Stress & Depression:
- Sad face, slow movements, unkempt look, drastic weight change (either up or down, assuming no other issues, such as cancer, thyroid problems or poor eating habits, exist).
- Feeling sad, hopeless, discouraged, and useless.
- Negative thoughts.
- Reduced creativity and pleasure in usual activities.
- People problems.
- Physical problems. Sleeping problems decreased sexual interest, headaches.
- Guilt and low self-esteem.
- Feeling worthless.
- Lack of future orientation in conversations.

What You Can Do To Cope With Stress:
- Revamp your spiritual life. Remember that God 'is a very present help in times of trouble.'
- Talk with family, brainstorm.
- Recall what you did in previous difficult circumstances.
- Maintain a sense of humor.
- Take one day at a time.
- Use innate problem-solving skills.
- Accept predicament over which you have no control.
- See the positive side of things.
- Use community resources such as accountant, guidance counselor, minister.

- Make time daily to unwind and focus one-on-one with each family member.
- Ask spouse for backrub; go to the spa; massage therapy, exercise.
- Stop, step back, and think. They say that hindsight is 20-20. Ask what do we really want for ourselves, for the person, and with the person with whom we are angry?
- Make a list of our strengths and accomplishments and enjoy them.
- Visit a trusted counselor, physician, and psychologist.

We must be alive to realize the vision to victory. Unfortunately, some people tend to overeat, or eat the wrong foods. Such practices open doorways for a myriad of health-related and other issues that militate against realization of the victory. For that reason, I would like to briefly discuss the values of proper nutrition and exercise from both the biblical and conventional perspectives.

# Chapter 11

## Proper Nutrition

A very elusive impediment to our victory is food. We need to eat to replenish, nourish our bodies, and generate the molecule known as Adenosine Triphosphate (ATP). This molecule is the universal energy currency required for chemical, mechanical, and transport activities in all living things. Without this energy molecule, our hearts will not beat, our lungs will not expand or contract, our muscles will not move, and certain large molecules could not be transported in our bodies.

Unfortunately, some of us eat ourselves to death. Stand in front of a grocery store and take a look at the shoppers. You will notice that the children of obese couple who come in to shop are also usually obese. They eat whatever their parents eat.

We tend to overeat, under eat or eat the wrong foods. Science teaches us that there are 92 naturally occurring elements in nature. However, we only need about 25 or so of these elements to survive, four to six of which are of paramount importance. These are carbon, hydrogen, oxygen, nitrogen, sulfur, and phosphorus. Additionally, there are about 40-50 monomeric compounds that can be combined in various forms to make polymers or macromolecules such as carbohydrates, lipids, proteins, and nucleic acids that form the major food groups with which we are familiar.

When we eat too much or eat the wrong foods (28) trouble sets into our bodies. These troubles can overwhelm us in the form of diseases and sicknesses. If not properly handled, these could shorten our lives.

It is believed that poor choice of foods may be correlated to certain aggressive behaviors or the high crime rate especially in low-income communities, and among repeat offenders. In other words, we are what we eat. Because of these and other reasons, I would like to provide a brief summary on nutrition from both religious and secular perspectives.

From the beginning, God has given us foods that can help prevent cancer and heart disease (Genesis 1: 29).

We know from these scriptures that God provided Adam and Eve with abundant fruits and vegetables. We can deduce from this premise that God probably intended for them to be vegetarians.

However, we learned that later when Adam and Eve tasted the forbidden fruit of the tree of the knowledge of good and evil, God allowed them to eat meat.

Another point of interest in the scriptures is that before the onset of the flood described in Genesis 7:2, a distinction arose between clean and unclean animals. Moses subsequently wrote biblical laws that distinguished between clean and unclean meat.

These Mosaic laws were based to some extent on their wholesomeness as food and on spiritual considerations. The scriptures presented the following foods as "clean":

**Clean foods in the Bible**

Leviticus 11:2-3   Clean, lean meat from certain animals. "Whatsoever parteth the hoof, and is cloven-footed, and cheweth the cud, among the beasts, that shall ye eat."

Leviticus 11:9; Deuteronomy 14:9. Fish with scales.

Proverbs 24:13; Deuteronomy 8:8; Genesis 43:11. Ingredients in honey are known to have several healing values.

The Book of Ruth 1:22. Barley grains.

Genesis 43:11. Almonds and other nuts are loaded with various nutrients.

Ezekiel 4:9 Millet.

Numbers 11:5. Cucumbers, leeks, melons, and onions.

Deuteronomy 8:8. Barley, wheat, grapes, and pomegranates.

Exodus 12:8, 15. Dark grainy bread is high in fiber and gives protection from both heart disease and cancer.

Ezekiel 4:9. Isaiah 7:15-22; Proverbs 27:27. Yogurt, milk of cows, sheep, and goats.

Genesis 25:34; Ezekiel 4:9. Beans and lentils

Numbers 11:5. Garlic contains cancer-fighting chemicals and helps maintain a good cholesterol level in the body.

Deuteronomy 8:8. Olive oil, which can "clean" the artery walls and strengthens the immune system.

Leviticus 11:22; Mark 1:6. Foods Considered "Unclean."

Leviticus 11:10. This list includes shellfish such as lobster and crab. These sea creatures are high in zinc and contain large amounts of cholesterol.

Deut.14: 21; Exodus 22:31. This list includes wild birds and scavengers. They feed on dead animals. About twenty-four species of birds were included in this category. Deuteronomy 14:21: "Ye shall not eat of any thing that dieth of itself," and in Exodus 22:31, the Hebrews were instructed, "neither shall ye eat any flesh that is torn of beasts in the field."

Leviticus 11:7. Pork and related products are described as unhealthy. The fats in these products contain saturated lipids that are hard to digest and may contribute to arteriosclerosis. Furthermore, they are carriers of pathogenic agents if not cooked or stored properly.

Leviticus 11:23. "But all other flying creeping things (besides locust, bald locust, beetle, and grasshopper), which have four feet, shall be an abomination unto you." Snakes are included in this category (Leviticus 11:41-43.

The reader should note that Yahshua (Jesus) abolished the distinction between clean and unclean foods (Mark 7:18-19), thus making all meats clean.

It is conventional wisdom that as long as we bless our food, the food is cleansed. However, it will also be wise for the reader to know that merely blessing food items do not remove the health risks such as cholesterol or poor nutritional value from them. As such, moderate consumption of such items is a great idea.

Let us not defile our bodies with poor choice of foods because by so doing we bring destruction to our bodies.

Let us be careful regarding overeating, under eating, poor choice of foods, and lack of rest, lack of exercise, worry, stress, and frustration. Such things are all potentially dangerous. There is scientific evidence that people who are subjected to sustained stress die prematurely. Overeating leads to obesity with implications on cardiovascular disease.

Lack of exercise. The Bible says in I Timothy 4:8 that "Bodily exercise profiteth little." Spiritual exercise is much more important, but it is important to exercise one's body whether it is walking, swimming, rollerblading, or lifting weights.

Not washing hands properly. By not performing this simple act one is contributing to the leading cause of diseases being spread all over the world. Many illnesses could be reduced or eliminated if one develops the habit of washing one's hands properly, especially after using the bathroom. The Bible talked about this simple action thousands of years ago in Deuteronomy 23:11.

In addition, it has been shown that several forms of bacteria such as E. coli and other foreign pathogenic agents can be spread by both children and adults through coughing or blowing their noses then touching a door handle, currency, or shaking hands.

## The Major Food Groups

Below is a brief overview of the major food groups needed for survival (1). This discussion covers certain benefits of each ingredient, including the functions and use of vitamins and food supplements.

You may be wondering why I am providing all this information on nutrition. It is important to eat healthy and maintain a healthy lifestyle so one could better enjoy life with one's spouse and family.

## Fats

Fats contain roughly twice as much energy as carbohydrates. It is recommended that caloric fat intake should be less than 30% of one's ideal caloric level. Fat contains approximately 9 calories per gram. Fats serve as storage forms of energy in the liver and adipose tissues. In addition, they provide insulation against heat loss and serve as cushions for vital organs.

It is important to know the calorie formula for weight loss purposes: 4086 (454gms X 9 cal/gm) calories equals approximately 1 pound of fat. In order to lose one pound of fat in one week, our body must (each day) burn 584 calories less than we consume as food (14). Only about 40% of the energy in the foods we consume is captured and stored for use later in the bonds of ATP. Some estimates of energy conversion are as low as 25%.

Assuming you bought a hamburger from a local restaurant that might contain approximately 35 grams of fat. Then multiply 35g x 9 cal/g = 315 calories. Assuming our overall caloric intake for that particular day was 3,000 calories, divide 3000 c / 315c = 9.52%. This means we are about 1/3 of the way from our total daily fat intake. There are three types of fats: saturated, monounsaturated, and polyunsaturated.

It is better to eat diets low in saturated fat. Such diets reduce the risk of arteriosclerosis and some forms of cancer. Examples of such diets include low fat or nonfat dairy products, egg substitutes, nuts and legumes (beans), corn, and safflower oils. Our intake of saturated fats should be 10% or less of our total caloric intake. An easy way to tell if a fat is saturated - if the fat is solid at room temperature then, it is saturated.

Foods that contain monounsaturated fat may protect against heart disease. Foods high in monounsaturated fat include olives, olive oil, avocados, and mayonnaise. Our intake of monounsaturated fats should be 10% or less of our total caloric intake.

Polyunsaturated fats provide limited protection against heart disease without providing excess fat. Foods high in polyunsaturated fat include tub margarine, safflower and sunflower oils, sunflower seeds, fish, and walnuts. Your intake of polyunsaturated fats should be 10% or less of your total caloric intake. Fats come from two main sources - animal sources and plant sources:

Limiting fat from animal sources is good because a diet low in animal fat generally reflects a diet low in saturated fat and cholesterol, which may help reduce our risk for heart disease and certain cancers.

Fish is a good, generally low fat source of protein containing mostly unsaturated fats. Including fish in your diet also provides omega-3 fatty acids, which may be helpful in preventing heart disease. Remember to use added fats sparingly when you are preparing fish.

Some fat is needed in the diet. Plant fat is less saturated than animal sources of fat and may contribute less to heart disease and cancer. Some plant fats, however, such as coconut oil and palm oil, are high in saturated fat and should be limited! Vegetable oils, nuts, tub margarine, and seeds are a good source of plant fat to include in your diet.

## Carbohydrates

It is recommended that our calories from carbohydrates should be within 55-80% of our ideal caloric level (28). Carbohydrates contain approximately 4 calories per gram. Consuming carbohydrates at this level helps provide the vitamins, minerals, and fiber we need for an active lifestyle. It is desirable to include generous amounts of complex carbohydrates, such as whole grains, pasta, and cereals and to limit added sugars to 10% or less of our total caloric intake.

We may follow the foregoing formula used for total fat intake but substitute 4 calories per gram instead of 9 calories per gram.

Complex carbohydrates are our body's preferred and best-utilized energy source. A low carbohydrate intake also decreases our likelihood of getting enough fiber in your diet. Foods high in complex carbohydrates/natural sugars include breads, cereals, grains, pastas, fruits, vegetables, and dried beans.

Since sugar contributes no nutrients other than calories and often travels with fat, a low intake is positive. By limiting the amount of sugar foods in our diet, we leave room for foods that have nutrients as well as calories.

It is recommended that we avoid or limit high sugar foods such as regular soft drinks, desserts, cookies, frozen desserts such as ice cream or ice milk, flavored yogurts, and sweetened cereals.

On food labels, the terms dextrose, sucrose, high fructose corn syrup, honey, maple syrup, and molasses all indicate added sugars. Our intake of simple sugars should be 10% or less of our total caloric intake.

### Protein

Our protein intake should be between 10%-20% of our total caloric intake. Proteins contain approximately 4 calories per gram. Too much protein strains our kidneys and may cause us to lose calcium. Protein consumed in excess of the amount we need is stored in our body as fat.

High protein foods include beef, pork, chicken, fish, nuts, dried beans, and dairy products. A three-ounce portion of meat, which is a recommended serving size, is about the size of a deck of cards. To calculate our total protein intake, we simply follow the formula used for total fat intake above, but substitute 4 calories per gram instead of 9 calories per gram.

There are two sources of protein: animal sources and plant sources.

Animal sources of protein are more complete than plant sources; however, they also commonly contain cholesterol and higher levels of saturated fat than plant sources. A high proportion of protein in the diet may crowd out foods high in carbohydrate (vegetables and grains), which are our best source of energy and contain other nutrients our body needs. Our intake of animal protein should be 50% or less of our total protein intake.

Plant sources include nuts, grains, and seeds. They have no cholesterol and have less saturated fat than animal sources of protein. Our intake of plant protein should be 50% or more of our total protein intake. To get all of the required amino acids necessary for a complete protein we can eat beans and rice or cornbread and beans

## Water

Water is a very essential nutrient for the body. Cells comprise anywhere from 70 to 95% water. Water has several unique qualities that make it so universally important for living things. Examples of these attributes include adhesiveness, cohesiveness, high specific heat, and high latent heat of vaporization, polarity, good solvent, and moderation of temperature. Water flushes impurities out of your body and helps your body to absorb vitamins more readily.

Filtered bottled water is necessary these days with all of the toxins in the tap water. Therefore accompany a well-balanced diet with water and a good multi-vitamin to make up for the lack of minerals. Current recommendations are to drink 8 or more eight ounce glasses of water a day.

## Fiber

Fiber is extremely important to the human body. It allows foods to digest properly and flow smoothly through the digestive tract. Most fibrous materials will hold approximately three times their weight in water. It has been suggested that a person's diet should contain at least 30 grams of dietary fiber a day.

Substituting whole grain breads and cereals for refined cereals and flour, legumes for red meat, fruits for sweet desserts, and adding salads on a daily basis easily accomplish this.

While the foregoing statement is acceptable, it has also been suggested that too much fiber, however, may cause poor absorption of vitamins and minerals and lead to nutritional deficiencies. Too much of anything might not be good for us. For example, too much fiber may also cause intestinal discomfort, bloating, diarrhea, and cramping. Fiber fills us, but it does not fatten us.

I will encourage the reader to invest in a blender as a way of increasing their fruit and fiber intake. For breakfast, I recommend that the reader blend his or her favorite fruits with an appropriate choice of juice in a blender. This practice would not only increase one's intake of fruit, fiber, minerals, and natural vitamins. It would help keep one's bowel movements regular. A lot of literature is available on the benefits of fruit and fiber consumption.

Fruits and vegetables provide nutrients essential for growth and renewal. They contain generous amounts of vitamins, which regulate metabolism and help in the conversion of fats and carbohydrates into energy.

Fruits and vegetables are major dietary sources of minerals. These minerals might be essential for proper nerve and muscle function. In addition, they could serve as building materials for some body tissue.

Fruits and vegetables can protect the body from such major diseases as cancer and heart disease because they contain substances known as anti-oxidants. These substances include beta-carotene, Vitamin C, E, and selenium. These substances also provide protection for cell membranes from the damage of free radicals.

An adequate intake of vitamin A insures proper night vision and healthy skin. Vitamin A may decrease your risk of some forms of cancer. Including a variety of vegetables such as carrots, spinach, broccoli, winter squash, and other dark green leafy vegetables will provide a continuous amount of vitamin A.

Similarly, an adequate intake of vitamin C (also known as ascorbic acid) will help our body resist infection and improves wound healing. Including fruits such as strawberries, green peppers, oranges, grapefruit, kiwi fruit, broccoli, cabbage, and lemons will help insure adequate intake of vitamin C. Vitamin C also acts as an anti-oxidant. It aids in the absorption of iron by the body. Please note: high levels of stress and exposure to second hand smoke will reduce our body's storage of vitamin C.

Potassium helps maintain our body's water balance and perform other functions. Examples of foods that are rich in this mineral include legumes (beans), whole grains, oranges, bananas, leafy vegetables, broccoli, potatoes, and meats.

Iron is often lacking in diets but is needed in minute amounts. It is usually bound to a protein component in blood and helps with the transportation of oxygen. Examples of foods rich in iron include lean red meats, mustard greens, kale, and fortified breads and cereals. They provide ample iron for a healthy diet. Calcium is also essential for proper bone growth and development. Good sources of calcium include low fat and nonfat dairy products, broccoli, mustard greens, and kale.

Phosphorus is essential in maintaining healthy bones and teeth. Phosphorus also functions in the breakdown of food for energy. Good sources of phosphorus include lean meats, low fat and nonfat dairy products, low fat baked products, and nuts.

A diet high in sodium can lead to water retention and high blood pressure. Many processed foods such as frozen dinners, canned vegetables, soups, and luncheon meats are high in sodium. When purchasing these types of foods, choose lower sodium versions. Selecting unprocessed fruits, vegetables, and whole grains will help keep your sodium intake within the recommended range.

It is important for the reader to be aware of certain elements that could adversely affect human health.

Alcohol in excess impairs judgment and damages the liver. From a caloric perspective, alcohol contains approximately 7 calories per gram. You can gain unwanted pounds quickly; yet receive no nutritional value from these empty calories because alcohol contains zero nutrients.

Caffeine is a substance unnecessary for good health and may actually be detrimental in larger quantities. Caffeine has been shown to cause complications during pregnancy, contribute to osteoporosis in women, increase hyperactivity in children, and cause mood swings.

MSG (monosodium glutamate) is known to trigger migraine headache, tachycardia, arrhythmia, seizures, asthma, nausea and vomiting, hives, skin rash, anxiety attacks, depression and much, much more in people who have become sensitive to it (28). It causes gross obesity and learning disorders in laboratory animals that ingest it when young. MSG is often used to increase the flavor sensation in foods

Aspartame (phenylalanine) is not healthy for humans. After consumption, the body converts aspartame to methanol, formic acid, and formaldehyde (the same substance used to embalm animals for purposes of scientific study). The last two of the three poisons, formaldehyde and formic acid, are suspected carcinogens.

Barley green is rapidly becoming North America's leading health drink. That is because barley green's nutritional profile is one of the best: Barley green contains the widest range of vitamins and minerals. Barley green is processed using a patented low-temperature, spray-drying process, so that the nutrients and the important enzymes remain intact.

When we consume Barley green, we are getting a "live" drink, full of the green goodness of barley grass. Of all the green grass juices, barley green is recognized as the world's leading food supplement, capturing various nutrients in a convenient and easy-to-use powder or caplet form.

Juices contain all of the goodness of the whole product in a condensed form. juicing fruits and vegetables quickly assimilate nutrients, since the body does not have to separate the fiber. Juices should be used as replacements for non-nutritious beverages such as soda, coffee, or alcohol.

In preparation for bottling, fruits and vegetables are usually heated and otherwise processed. These processes cause the loss of vitamins, minerals, trace elements, and enzymes. Fresh fruit and vegetable juices that are extracted and consumed shortly thereafter experience a minimum amount of nutrient loss.

Drinking juices can have many therapeutic benefits; however, juicing is not recommended to take the place of medical treatment, but as an adjunct to treatment.

In addition, since fruit juice is high in natural sugars, those who have been advised to limit their sugar intake should use it sparingly. This may include individuals who have diabetes, hypoglycemia, candidiasis, and gout.

The best way to lose weight is to eat enough food to supply calories within your ideal caloric range, limit saturated fat and simple sugars, and increase our activity level. Under eating, is not the answer, it may make us more prone to health problems, lessen our resistance to disease, or give us headaches. A low calorie intake may cause us to feel tired and may lead to binge eating due to hunger.

The Atkins diet named after its deceased founder has been a popular diet fad in recent times. It promotes high protein which has an adverse effect on the kidneys over a prolonged use (14). A certain diet has recently received a lot of notoriety. This diet encourages an individual to eat all of the fat and protein he or she wants in a meal while avoiding all forms of carbohydrate. However, it is important to note that carbohydrates, especially complex carbohydrates, are essential.

People who are on this diet do not get the fiber, vitamins, and minerals from carbohydrates, which are needed for healthy living; but rather does much harm to our arteries by taking large amounts of saturated fat and harm our kidneys by eating large amounts of protein.

It is known that certain vitamin or mineral deficiencies can lead to certain health deficiencies (28), such as:

## Fatigue

According to a study cited in the Journal of Nutritional Medicine, the most common symptom of a vitamin B12 deficiency is fatigue. Thiamine has also been found to help with fatigue. Eating sugar will cause thiamine depletion as will smoke tobacco products and drinking alcohol.

Sleeping pills, sedatives, and tranquilizers can contribute to poor quality sleep. It is much better to go the natural route. Calcium (always combined with magnesium) helps relax the muscles and soothe the nerves. Magnesium also works with vitamin

B6 and tryptophan.

## Depression

Certain B vitamins have been found to be deficient in patients with severe depression. Limited clinical studies have shown injections of B12 with B-complex to relieve the symptoms of depression. Also, proper amounts of magnesium and potassium are necessary for good neurological health (14).

## Colds

Vitamin C (especially with bioflavonoid) helps reduce the severity of colds. You should take a vitamin C formula that uses lemon, grape, citrus, buckwheat, and green tea for bioflavonoid.

## Arthritis

Arthritis can be caused by food allergies. Common allergens are sugar, beef, chocolate, eggs, citrus fruits, coffee, corn, milk, malt, pork, soybeans, potatoes, spices, tomatoes, wheat, and yeast. Arthritis pain comes from swelling, so seek out foods containing natural anti-inflammatory agents. Curcumin (which gives turmeric its yellow color) has been found in studies to work better than ibuprofen.

## Acne

When it comes to curing acne, the answer is zinc.
The Bible says in **Hosea 4:6** that "people perish for lack of knowledge." By obtaining the knowledge from this teaching and applying it to our daily lifestyle, we will be on our way to living a healthier and more satisfying life for victory over ONE PLUS ONE EQUALS ONE.

## Aging

Aging is a syndrome of degenerative disease characterized by age related diseases such as cardiovascular dysfunction, cancer and arthritis. One of the primary causes of aging is oxidative stress from free radicals.

Through improper diet, external pollutants, stress of life, our body's cells are continually bombarded by millions of free radicals each day. The degree and the amount of free radicals present in the body are related directly to the speed of the aging process

Menopause and andropause are a normal natural aging process for females, and males respectively. As has been reported in the news recently, hormone substitutions in women increase their risk of cancer. Diets high in soy-isoflavonals show promise in reducing the symptoms of menopause while not affecting a woman's health (45).

A number of nutritional supplements may be useful for families, especially senior citizens. A few of these and their impacts on various physiological processes are listed below:

Cardiovascular System Protection:

- Ascorbyl Palmitate: 100 - 200 mg
- L-Lysine: 150 - 250 mg
- L-Proline: 100 - 200 mg
- Amylase: 1,500 SKBU
- Cellulase: 500 ECU
- Lipase: 4800 IU
- Ascorbic Acid (Vitamin C): 1,000 - 3,000 mg
- Coenzyme Q10: 30 - 120 mg
- L-Carnitine: 500 - 2,000 mg
- Lipoic Acid: 100 - 400 mg

Musculoskeletal System Protection:

a. Calcium: 500 mg
b. Magnesium: 400 - 1,000 mg
c. Malic Acid: 100 - 500 mg

d. The magnesium to calcium ratio should be at least 1 to 1. Some anti-aging researchers are advocating a ratio of 2 to 1.

Cancer Prevention:

   a. Calcium D-Glucarate: 100-300 mg
   b. Vitamin E: 400 - 800 IU
   c. Beta-Carotene: 15,000 - 30,000 IU
   d. Grapeseed Extract: 50 - 100 mg
   e. Citrus Bioflavonoids: 50 - 150 mg
   f. Selenium: 200 - 400 mcg

People that live in the Mediterranean region have one of the lowest heart attack rates in the world. Their diet consists of 50 percent complex carbohydrates (fruits and vegetables), 25 percent protein (from plant source like tofu and fish like salmon), and 25 percent fat (from fish and olive oil). Their saturated fats, refined carbohydrates, and sugar intake are very low. The Mediterranean diet is an excellent model for anti-aging diet.

Fruits and vegetables contain abundant antioxidants and phytonutrients. Fish contains essential fatty acids that are critical in building blocks of neurotransmitters and hormones. Moderate amount of plant-based protein such as soybean is easy on the digestive system compared to red or white meat.

Our diet should be fortified with digestive enzymes such as amylase, cellulose, and lipase, which may be needed to digest protein and enhance gastrointestinal heath. This should be part of the daily supplement intake. Reduction of sugar intake and avoidance of cigarette and alcohol are also important. Finally, a reduction of calories by 30 percent to achieve 5 to 10 percent below the ideal body weight should be considered.

## Proper Exercise

Exercise, in addition to its cardiovascular benefits, also increases the level of hormones in the body, which include growth hormone, testosterone, DHEA and pregnenolone. Performing strength-training exercise is a key component to an anti-aging exercise program because of the above-mentioned effects. Without a doubt, exercise is the closest thing to the anti-aging magic bullet as one can get. Those who exercise regularly live longer. It's that simple.

One of the interesting facts of diet and nutrition is called the European paradox (14). Many diets in Europe are high in fat yet the rate of heart disease is lower than in the US. Several things contribute to this seemingly backward finding.

1. Europeans eat their salad as the last course of a meal. This speeds up the passage of food through the intestinal tract causing less time for food to be absorbed and lowering the total quantity of calories obtained from the food.
2. Europeans eat their meals slowly and usually around the same time of day (3-4 hours before bed time). This allows satiety (a feeling of fullness) and also allows the small intestines empty before bedtime when body functions slow down.
3. Europeans walk or ride bicycles to work or play more than Americans. This increases their fitness which aids in weight control.
4. Sadly, a study of Japanese immigrants who while still in Japan had a lower rate of heart disease, has shown that after a few years in the US, their rate of heart disease is equal to that of a native-born citizen.

## Stressful Professions

Hans Selya wrote a book several years ago about stress and how humans react to stressful situations. In his book he emphasized the importance that both good stress (eustress) and bad stress (stress) have the same effect on the body. Namely, it depletes the body's ability to fight or resist disease. In psychology classes, students are introduced to a test that evaluated a persons potential to get sick after being exposed to stress.

An example in the book says that if you have a major life event like a divorce it can increase the likelihood that you will have a major illness within 1 year (14). Many healthcare professionals feel that stress of daily living in America's fast pace economy is a major cause of illness. This also contributes greatly to heart disease, mental illness, depression and many other ailments.

Some jobs are more stress prone than others. For example, police officers, firefighters, air-traffic controllers, and persons working rotating shifts at manufacturing plants are more likely to have increased numbers of sick days than those in less stressful job situations like gardeners.

Exercise is the best way to relieve stress and the least harmful. People who avoid exercise are also the ones who need medications to sleep, then for alertness at work. Thus, we are becoming an over medicated society.

Another important component of the vision for victory is the need to properly raise and position our children for success. It must be one of the greatest joys of victorious $21^{st}$ century families to see their children grow up, and hopefully become more successful than the previous generations. Success does not come knocking at our doors. Some are born with silver spoons in their mouth. Others find success through various ways by their God-given talents, being at the right place at the right time, marrying into a successful family, or remotely by winning the lottery.

Unfortunately, our children are exposed to tremendous amounts of pressure from various sources both within and without the family unit. I would like to briefly touch on some of these factors, their possible impacts on our youth, and then present positive information on how to increase the chances for success among our youth.

A part of responsible victorious parenting, among other things, must include sharing of positive experiences, and providing proper guidance to our youth. The Holy Spirit has revealed 14 success attributes that must be instilled into our children to help encourage, motivate, and position them for success. These attributes are presented in the chapter that follows.

# Chapter 12

## Positioning the Children of Victorious 21$^{st}$ Century Families for Success

Our children are our future. As responsible parents, we must do all we can to position them properly in order to change their outcome for success. This is a major element in the vision for victorious 21$^{st}$ Century families.

In certain parts of the world, a fantastic job of caring for children is done successfully. However, during the adolescent years, many parents fail to realize that those are probably the most crucial years in the lives of their children, at least in helping to prepare them for their future.

Due in part to various physiological changes at puberty, transition from elementary to high school, and other factors, children become adventurous and experimental. It was not known until recently that an increase in brain cells occur around this time. If such cells are used, the child keeps them. If not, they are lost. In essence, mother nature provides a mechanism to help children during puberty prepare themselves for their future.

These are the critical times when parents must observe and work with their children in establishing their future. As the Bible says, we must raise our children in the way they should go, and when they grow up, they will not depart from that.

Unfortunately, the outward manifestations of these changes unfortunately are misconstrued as rebelliousness, even though they might well be so in some cases. For instance, parents fail to establish inbound or out of bound parameters for fear that their children might hate them, desire for the children to develop some independence or for other reasons.

As such, the situations are not corrected responsibly and/or in concert with their teachers in schools. Eventually, there arise difficulties that sometimes lead to unpleasant situation for the student or parent. Some of the difficulties might be that some children register in colleges absolutely unprepared or undecided in their major field of study.

Sometimes, they become problems to their instructors. For those who do not go to college or trade school, they enter the work force not having a clue what the real world really holds for them. Despite these difficulties, some children, manage to succeed.

In other parts of the world, parents believe there must be continuity in training and preparing their children for the real world. I have seen grown men and women, some married with children still living with their parents.

God wants parents to have some mechanism in place to pass on good experiences to their children so they do not repeat the mistakes of their parents. Imagine the creation of daycare or recreational centers where retired professionals volunteer their time sharing their experiences in certain modified forms to our youth. What a worthwhile investment that would be!

Of course, this might not be appealing to middle-to-high income stable families. Such families can choose to place their children in private schools. However, most of our children come from dysfunctional homes. A major problem of dysfunctional or in some cases stable homes, is child abuse.

## Child Abuse

Previously, I discussed the impacts of relationship breakdown, and family violence on children. I would like to revisit the topic of abuse from a different perspective. This problem is rampant. For that reason, I would like to use reliable references from selected countries to drive home this message. The incidence of child abuse and neglect also seems related to dysfunctional relationship.

The Australian Institute of Health and Welfare concluded 30,615 substantiated cases of child abuse and neglect, involving 26,544 children, was reported in 1994-95 (25).

Stepchildren were involved in 21 per cent of cases, although less than 4 per cent of children lived in stepfamilies. Although 81 per cent of children lived with biological parents, they accounted for only 30 per cent of cases.

Dr Neville Turner of the National Children's Bureau of Australia estimated that a child whose mother lived in a de facto relationship with a man other than the child's father, or with a husband that is not the child's father, was at least five times more likely to be abused than one who lives with both married parents.

Of 86 homicide victims aged under 15 years from 1989-92, 60 were likely to be killed by parents or de facto parents; three by other family members; 12 by acquaintances; and only three by strangers. In another study, it was reported that a high proportion of child killers are either stepfathers or the mother's de facto husband or boyfriend.

Dr Ania Wilczynski found that non-biological parents present "a disproportionate risk for children, particularly in the early stages of their relationship with the children." The proportion of suspected killers in de facto relationships was 6.5 times higher than for the general population. The study found that 28 per cent of the child killers had become parents at age 20 or younger.

### Youth homelessness

According to the National Inquiry into Youth Homelessness, family conflict, including violence and abuse, is one of the major factors leading to youth homelessness in Australia ( 25) .

It has been suggested that there are up to 250,000 young people not living with their families, and that approximately 30 per cent of 15-20 year olds are living independently from their families and are vulnerable to drifting in and out of homelessness.

According to a Victorian study, there are about 11 in every 1,000-school children who are homeless. Children aged between the ages 5 and 18 made more than four million calls to the Kids Help Line between 1991 and 1995. There were 120,744 calls classified as serious, of which 44,554 (36.5 per cent) concerned relationship problems. Half of that number was about family relationships. Most of the callers were under 16, and three quarters
of them girls.

In the United States, Sara McLanahan (23), herself a single parent, and professor of sociology at Princeton University, concluded her detailed analysis of four major national studies of families – three of them longitudinal:

Children who grow up in a household with only one biological parent are worse off, on average, than children who grow up in a household with both of their biological parents, regardless of the parent's race or educational background, regardless of whether the parents are married when the child is born, and regardless of whether the resident parent remarries.

McLanahan did not claim that single parenthood was the only reason that some children do poorly: income, parenting patterns, neighborhood resources, and educational level are all factors, but they are boosted by the absence of a parent.

The non-partisan Council on Families in America, comprising leading scholars of both conservative and liberal inclinations, concluded in their report on marriage:

The evidence continues to mount, and it points to one striking conclusion: the weakening of marriage has had devastating consequences for the well-being of children. To be sure, television, the movies, and popular music contribute to declining child well-being.

So do poor teaching, the loss of skilled jobs, inefficient government bureaucracies, meager or demeaning welfare programs, and the availability of guns and drugs.

By far the most important causal factor is the remarkable collapse of marriage, leading to growing family instability and decreasing parental investment in children.

The renowned family scholar, Professor Urie Bronfenbrenner stated in a 1994 seminar: "There has been progressive disarray at an accelerating rate of the disorganization of the family in the western world. Children are better off economically, psychologically, emotionally with both parents. In addition, fathers (despite their bad press) are an important resource for their children's well-being. Step-families are a high risk, even though, financially, children are better off if the custodial parent re-marries."

Some of the readers of ONE PLUS ONE EQUALS ONE are quite likely to have formulated their opinions about life. I think I can make some inroad into changing their mindset, and equip them with certain attributes that could help them help themselves in positioning their children in their attitudes, thereby change the outcome for success of their children.

Allow me to take you on an imaginary journey to a city called ONE PLUS ONE EQUALS ONE. Using our creative faculties and sanctified imagination, let us begin to see ourselves riding on an air-conditioned tour bus. Do not worry about directions to the City of ONE PLUS ONE EQUALS ONE. I will do the driving.

Within a few hours, we arrive at the gates to the city. But, before we enter this city called ONE PLUS ONE EQUALS ONE, I ought to tell you something about the inhabitants of this city.

You will not find depression, poor anger control, and teenage suicide among the youth of this city. You will not find young children taking anti-depressants. Such drugs lead to the development of suicidal tendencies.

Peer pressure, Lack of Virtue, and Improper Character Education are unheard of in this city. Let me assure the parents among our group to be at ease and mingle with the youth in the City of ONE PLUS ONE EQUALS ONE . The youth are respectful, especially of the elderly.

You will find a lot of handsome young women and young men here but do not worry about their co-mingling, because they dress appropriately, have virtue, high self-esteem, and do not engage in teenage sex. Look at their fingers. You will find them wearing promissory rings that signify they are saving themselves for their spouses when the right time comes for them to get married. Before I forget, I would like to inform you that the youth of the City of ONE PLUS ONE EQUALS ONE has good planning and goal-setting skills, combined with a low high school dropout rate.

Allow me to tell you that you will not find idle minds in this city. As you roam about the city on Sunday morning, you will find the spiritual head of each household leading their families to church. Because birds of a feather flock together, these unique people have inculcated a sense of identity, a sense of dependency upon one another, and a tendency to acquire and use recent technology to further the prosperity of their city.

We are now at City Hall. The mayor has come to welcome us. We express to the mayor how impressed we are with his affluent city. Suddenly, someone in the audience gets curious. He asks the mayor how he has managed to mold the city of ONE PLUS ONE EQUALS ONE to near perfection. The following is the mayor's response:

"My brothers and sisters, there are fourteen attributes (2) we continually instill in the youth of the city of ONE PLUS ONE EQUALS ONE. These principles have become part of the lives of the adults in this city.

We have come to discover that development of these attributes helps one know himself and seek self-improvement; develop a sense of responsibility; make sound and timely decisions; be an example to others; seek responsibility, and take responsibility for one's actions.

They prepare you to be the head and not the tail later on in life. Let us take a closer look at these attributes:

1. Truthfulness. This builds positive fields around you. Tell the truth even if it is not easy. Telling lies opens doors for the past to linger on into the future. You might find yourself watching your back or loosing sleep needlessly. Telling the truth closes door of the past while ushering in pleasant things in the future.

Positive values will guide your choices such as developing a sense of helping other people, accepting and taking personal responsibility for your actions and knowing that it is inappropriate to be sexually active, or use drugs or alcohol.

These values additionally attract the right people such as your family members, neighbors, non-parent, responsible, and Godly adults in your community.

This is what the African adage, "It takes an entire village to raise a child" means! Remember, it has been said that, "A family that prays together, stays together."

For the purposes of ONE PLUS ONE EQUALS ONE, let us re-phrase that to say, "A family that prays together must stay together to raise successful children." This is critical in the upbringing of our youth, because of high divorce rates; geographical separation of extended family; both parents working outside home, the majority of children elsewhere are being influenced by irresponsible peers rather than Godly adults.

For this reason, hold fast the word of God. Proverbs 3: 1-2 states, "My son, forget not my law; but let thine heart keep my commandments; for length of days, and long life, and peace, shall they add to thee." In that regard, we encourage our youth to communicate effectively and positively with their parents.

Proverbs 1:8-9 states, "My son, hear the instruction of they father, and forsake not the law of thy mother; they shall be ornaments of grace unto thy head, and chains about thy neck." We encourage our youth to seek advice and counsel from their parents.

2. Recognize the opportunities in your circumstance. Blessings sometimes come in disguise. No matter what difficulties our children face, we teach them to always find opportunities associated with those circumstances. For example, loss of a job later on in life might present an opportunity to pursue another career. They realize they are not alone in whatever difficulty they face.

Our youth identifies and affiliates with organizations and institutions that provide positive, supportive environments. Organizations such as the Young Men's Christian Association (YMCA)/Young Women Christian Association (YWCA) have helped many.

Yes, we encourage them to take advantage of facilities, amenities, and professional staff provided by their schools. It is important for parents to get involved in their children's schooling. It is the responsibility of the parents to ensure that they know acceptable or unacceptable behaviors. It is part of responsible parenting. This gets them out of a lot of trouble, and helps them succeed.

The success of our youth depends in part on a positive environment established by their parents. They cannot leave the upbringing their children to your teachers. Rather the parents must work in partnership with the teachers.

Working together, they must set clear and comprehensible rules including failure to comply with such rules; know where their children are, especially at night; model positive, responsible behavior; and encourage them to do well in school.

3. Education. We believe that knowledge is power. Educate your children on whatever circumstance they face. Education is a key element to their success. They will be more able to tolerate the uncertainties of life if they understand the underlying factors. They must know and understand the causes and effects of their actions.

The level of their education will determine their income, and where they will live in the future. Thus, we motivate them to make a commitment to learning while time is on their side.

I am not saying that parents must turn their children into 'book worm.' The children must develop a study table, and let the children around you buy into that. If they assimilate information systematically, they will be able to recall information systematically, too. We have found it helpful in avoiding drawing blanks during exams.

Outside of their study periods, our children engage in extracurricular activities such as music, theatre, sports, and organizations at their school or place of worship. They find time to be with their friends with nothing special to do. Consider the following example.

The highest amount of money made by people who work at food stands or greeters at major department stores without adequate education make is about $12,000 annually. If we take into account the cost of rent, utilities, food, car, car insurance, clothing, etc. we will discover that a person can barely live on that for only a few months. That is not success! That could lead us in situations we would not like to find ourselves in.

One might say, "My child does not like....school is boring...this or that subject is too hard ...I don't like this teacher."

Proverbs 16:3 "Commit thy works unto the Lord, and thy thoughts shall be established." Why? Because Proverbs 16:25 states that, "There's a way that seemeth right unto a man, but the end thereof are ways of death." Encourage your children to seek what God's plan is for them.

If they make this commitment, God will faithfully establish their paths to success. That is why it is very crucial to stay within the Divine Blueprint for marriage and family relations. The Bible says, "All things work for the good of those who love the Lord, and who are called according to His purpose."

Once they know what God's plan is for them, they must take the initiative to motivate themselves to do well in school, especially in the sciences. Remember, Oprah Winfree's father made her read many books, as a teenager. That is the way of the future.

We encourage our children to engage actively in learning. Proverbs 4:7 states: "Wisdom is the principal thing; therefore get wisdom; and with all thy getting get understanding."

4. Courage. It takes courage to admit one's faults or stand up for one's beliefs. Courage goes hand in hand with integrity. That means, one must have enough courage to act on one's conviction and stand up for one's beliefs.
If Rosa Parks in the United States had not exercised enough courage to stand up for what she believed in, families of people of African descent in the United States might still be riding at the back of city buses.

If the people who wrote the "Declaration of Independence" had been cowards, the British would have controlled the United States for a much longer time.

If Dr. Martin Luther King did not have courage and integrity, I do not know where families of people of African descent would be in terms of their civil rights, today.

5. Effective communication. We remind our youth that it is not their ability to speak well that matters. Rather, it is how well their audience understands what they are saying. Effective communication has its benefits. It helps you build good relationships; it helps you build trust, and settle your differences non-violently. Ps 37 "Fret not you because of evildoers...as the green herb."

I have known many young adults who got into fights and, therefore, in trouble at school because someone called them by a certain unacceptable name.

All people upon birth were given names by their parents. That is the only name they must answer to. Our children later finds out that good communications are essential to a successful marriage, and in other relations including the workplace.

6. Patience. In today's society, many factors have been created that tend to influence people to take possession of things they would like to have right away. Patience is no longer perceived as a virtue by many. However, it is, and must be. Ps. 40 teach that, "I waited patiently on the Lord....and He inclined unto me, and heard my cry."

Success does not always come when we want it to. To be patient, one must exert control over events and circumstances that come his/her way. That means one must remember one's life has a purpose. As such, no matter how difficult the wait seems to be, one must be optimistic about his/her future. We motivate our youth to be optimistic about their future (Ps. 23 "The Lord is my shepherd, I shall not want."

7. Follow your instincts and develop a passionate Commitment to the resolution of the issue at hand. By "instincts" I mean following our gut feelings. "Commitment" means doing what we enjoy doing.

8. Creativity. Teach your children to think outside the box. Find realistic more effective and plausible alternatives to circumvent their problem. Jesse Owens, a famous Olympic athlete, was taught by his mother to run as if the ground was on fire. Consequently, he won many races.

A famous baseball player also found a creative way to hit record setting home runs. At the time of his active competition, people of color were not allowed in stadiums. They were also mistreated in several other ways.

Yet, that athlete was allowed to entertain others who did not look like him. He wrote that he took his anger out not on people but on the baseball. He used all the energy he could muster to hit the baseball so hard that he made many home runs. That was an example of transferring negative to positive energy. Look within ourselves. We will find our own way to win our battles.

9. Faithfulness. There are many definitions of faith. The simplest one I know of is 'Belief transformed to experience'. That is faith. We convince our youth that their imaginations and visualizations will materialize, if they have faith in God and in themselves. That means they must be unwavering in their belief. They must maintain their focus on their ideals.

10. Persistence and consistence. We teach our children to be persistent and consistent in their quest to succeed. Remember someone else may have the same idea you have. Therefore, we must act on our ideas otherwise someone else would.

Our youth know that they should not start something worthwhile and not finish it. That means they must stay in school. They must be persistent in their desire not to give in to drugs, alcohol, pre-marital sex, and things of that nature.

11. Will. Having a will means when everyone says you cannot, you tell yourself that I can. When you are caught in a difficult situation you tell yourself, "I can do all things through Yahshua (Jesus) which strengthens me"

12. Strengths and weaknesses. Remind your children that they need not overestimate their strengths. Similarly, they should not underestimate their weaknesses either. King David overestimated his strength. He thought he could look, for just a little bit, at a woman bathing from his palace. Before he realized, he has become an adulterer and murderer.

On the other hand, Joseph knew what would happen if he spent time alone with Potifar's wife. Although that somehow got him in trouble, the truth ultimately prevailed, and he rose through the ranks to become prime minister of Egypt.

13. Inspiration. Motivate children to draw inspiration from others or be an inspiration to others themselves. Remember others have gone through the situation in which you or your children find yourself and have prevailed. There is nothing you will face that is new under the sun.

While in prison, Nelson Mandela drew inspiration from others. That helped him survive. Similarly, Dr. Martin Luther King, Jr. while in prison, drew inspiration from others including Mohandas Gandhi. That helped him survive his predicament. Their experiences have helped others in difficult situations overcome their ordeals.

14. Thankfulness. People remember when one shows appreciation and gratitude.

The mayor concluded that those fourteen principles are the secret to their success.

In addition to the above, other factors must be addressed as we continue our journey into the land "flowing with milk and honey," for $21^{st}$ century victorious families.

# Chapter 13

## Additional Impediments to Victory

Self-control, the love of money or greed, and control of the tongue (1) are three factors that God wants families to attend to, as we embark on this victorious journey.

## Self-Control

Some of our great leaders, especially men, must learn to control their sexual desires. More often than not, most men underestimate the power of a woman. Many evil deeds on earth have been committed because of greed or avarice.

The fact of the matter is that the marriage or families of the perpetrators or their progeny pay severe price for these actions eventually. One needs to examine the predicament of a famous family on the east coast of the United States, in the United Kingdom, and elsewhere, to have a good picture of the impact of these acts on their lives.

God created sexual intercourse for the propagation of the species and the earthly pleasure of legally married couples. However, the sexual instinct can sometimes overwhelm some men or women.

Like David in the Old Testament, many men overestimate their strength in resisting the power of a woman. This sometimes leads to disastrous consequences. They fail to recognize the ability of the enemy to use desires of the flesh to sidetrack God's plan in their lives.

I have previously discussed several physiological differences between the two genders. Let me reiterate that men and women differ physiologically, especially in their sexual instincts and desires. A woman comes into this world with the total number of eggs that could be fertilized already determined at conception. It might be zero, one, two, 100, etc.

Therefore, psychologically, a woman is 'programmed' to be conscious of who fertilizes her precious eggs. This is one reason why it takes women longer to get sexually involved or be ready for sexual intercourse, compared to men.

On the other hand, men produce millions of sperm cells that vie for the female egg. Only one is successful in locating and fertilizing the female egg. The remainder die or are reabsorbed. A man may produce viable sperm cells well into his old age. As such, there is no real concern to conserve the sperm cells.

God created woman to be a helpmate for man. It is the woman, rather than the man, who carries babies. However, most men have yet to learn how to control the desires of the flesh.

Another difficulty associated with sexuality is hidden in the genes. We know that normal males have 'X' and 'Y' chromosomes. Regular females carry two 'X' chromosomes. Sometimes certain abnormalities occur during the process of Meiosis (production of sperm and egg cells).

The two sex determinants (X, X or X, Y) must separate before union of the sperm and egg. However, a phenomenon known as "Nondisjunction" can sometimes occur which leads to failure of the chromosomes to separate. Thus, an individual could end up with "XXY" (Klinefelter syndrome). Such people usually have male sex organs. Furthermore, their testes tend to be very small and are often sterile.

Other characteristics include enlarged breasts and other feminine features. Males with "XYY" genotypes are usually taller than average. Females with "XXX" genotype cannot usually be distinguished from those with XX genotype. Additional studies should be done to verify if such conditions could be related to alternate life styles, especially in light of the HIV/AIDS pandemic.

A lot of credit has been given Gregor Mendel, Thomas Morgan and others for their work in genetics. We must not overlook the fact that long before these men walked the face of this earth King David already alluded to genetic principles such as transcription, translation, meiosis, and base pairing rules in Psalm 139.

Nevertheless, throughout history, and in the circular world, we learn that many great leaders have fallen from grace to grass by the hands of women, or have failed to accomplish their calling because they underestimated the power of women.

Recent examples include prominent televangelists, a prominent pastor who was recently released from jail in Florida, and a high profile Pastor of a large church right here in Houston. Many more incidents are bound to come out of the closet. A few examples from the Bible are provided below:

- Eve (Genesis 3: 1-7)
- Jael Heber's Wife (Judges 4: 9, 21)
- David and Bathsheba (II Samuel 11:2-5; 21; 15; 27)
- Abimelech, the son of Jerubesheth was slain by a woman who cast a piece of a millstone upon him from a wall (II Samuel 11: 21)
- Samson and Delilah (Judges 14:1; 16:17-19)
- King Solomon and Women (I Kings 11: 1)
- Queen Esther (Esther 7: 1-10)

## Money

They say that money is the root of all evil. However, there is no question that we all need money to live. Money by itself is not very bad. It is the love of money...greed, avarice, and when people tend to look upon money as their god rather than have Faith in El Elyon, the Almighty God, that creates problems for them. Money is just a resource. God gives people the ability to acquire wealth.

Plans made for the vision for the victory in ONE PLUS ONE EQUALS ONE must not overlook the use of Proverbs 15:22.

Money will be needed to fully implement the vision of ONE PLUS ONE EQUALS ONE. I know that it is the will of God for you and me to continue to embark on this journey to success. If we continue to walk with Him in faith, we will experience the financial blessings He had assured.

We must move in faith in every realm. Let us be reminded that our Faith in God must be valid, viable, and victorious. It is the uncompromising confidence in God's ability to perform His will in our behalf despite the opposition.

Application of the following principles could assist us to bring forth the harvest of finance and other blessings from God we so desperately need to get this worthy project off the ground (8). There are certain assumptions we must make:

- We must accept that our assignment is greater than our present financial situation. When Yahshua (Jesus) commanded the multitudes to be fed, the disciples did not have enough food to feed them. Their assignment exceeded the amount of money in the treasury. Nevertheless, that particular need was met miraculously.

- We must be reminded that the Living God specializes in the impossible. If this job is within our scope currently, it will not require our faith to accomplish it, and we would get the glory. However, if we perceive this assignment to be from God and He has to do it, then God will get the glory. Yes, the Bible teaches that, "But Yahshua (Jesus) beheld them, and said unto them, with men this is impossible; but with God all things are possible." With GOD on our side, we can make it.

- We must continually enter into the power of prayer. Jeremiah encourages us to call on God. We can pray and receive what we need. Yahshua (Jesus) taught in his model prayer to pray for provisions. Let us stand together on Faith in this endeavor. There is power in the prayer of agreement (Matthew 18:19).

- We must practice the laws of sowing and reaping. The bible teaches that if us sow bountifully, we will reap bountifully.

- We must maintain a biblical confession of faith for God's continued financial increase.

- Charity begins at home. Therefore, we must keep our houses in order. God says the natural is first and then the spiritual (I Corinthians 15).

- We need to align our vision with God's provision (Proverbs 29:18). If we are following the vision of the Lord, the Lord will give us a plan. Begin to follow others who have had success in releasing finances for ministry.

## Control of the Tongue

One major impediment that could stand between victory and us is the tongue. It is a power so great that it is capable of producing life or death depending on how it is used. God wants us to control our tongues. We were created in the image of God. Therefore, we have some of his attributes. Few people realize that miracles can come out of our mouth.

So powerful is the power of the tongue that it can bring to pass the intentions of God. In the Christian faith, it is believed that the world was created by the spoken word of God.

Yahshua's coming into the world had to be announced by divine inspiration, through the power of the Holy Spirit by the spoken word, to bring it to pass. Healing came to many through the power of the spoken word pronounced on them by Yashua.

Similarly, evil spirits need and can possess human bodies in order to have a mouth piece.

The Book of James teaches that,

"But the tongue can no man tame; it is an unruly evil, full of deadly poison. Therewith bless us God, even the Father; and therewith curse we men, which are made after the similitude (image) of God." (James 3:8-9)

Furthermore, we read in Proverbs 18:21 that, "Death and life are in the power of the tongue."

An example of how words can bring forth death and destruction can also be found in Mark 11:13-14, 20:

"And seeing a fig tree afar off having leaves, he Yahshua (Jesus)) came, if haply he might find any thing thereon: and when he came to it, he found nothing but leaves; for the time of figs was not yet. In addition, Yahshua (Jesus) answered and said unto it, No man eat fruit of thee hereafter forever. In addition, his disciples heard it. And in the morning, as they passed by, they saw the fig tree dried up from the roots."

On the other hand, an example of words bringing forth life can be found in John 11:43-44:

"And when He thus had spoken, Yahshua (Jesus) cried with a loud voice, Lazarus, come forth. In addition, he that was dead came forth, bound hand and foot with grave clothes: and his face was bound about with a napkin. Yahshua (Jesus) saith unto them, loose him, and let him go."

Words that come out of our mouths carry power. It has been reported by scientists that for every bad or destructive word our children hear, there must be at least 27 good or encouraging words to cancel out the adverse impacts of that word on the child in view. Therefore, our words carry power. Many people are suffering untold misery because of things they said, or things said to or about them by others. For this reason, we must continually say positive things in order to surround ourselves with positive people and positive things.

When reading the Gospels, you will notice that everything surrounding Yahshua (Jesus)' entire life (His birth, ministry, death, burial, and resurrection) was a direct fulfillment of the spoken word of God's prophets. Examples include the following Matthew 1: 22; 2:15; 2: 23.

You see, just as God Himself spoke the world into existence, we as believers in Yahshua speak forth our future (1,8). For this reason, we must know how to use the power of our tongues to speak positive things in our lives, and in the lives of others.

Another spiritual secret is that we must let our words be few. Some of us talk too much. We discuss our marital and family matters with almost every one. We fail to realize that we must wash our marital and family dirty linens at home rather than abroad.

At times, God has a plan for us but wishes to execute it secretly so that the enemy does not hinder the working of the plan. An example of that could be found in the instructions given Joshua for the conquest of Jericho (Joshua 6:10).

Also during His arrest, at the pronouncement of that name, the soldiers fell backwards under the power of the spoken name (John 18:5-6). Again, at His trial Yahshua could not even speak his name because it would have freed Him (8). That is why He remained silent.

The Bible tells in Ecclesiastes 5:2 to "let our words be few." Proverbs 13:3 says: "He that keepeth his mouth keepeth his life: but he that openeth wide his lips shall have destruction."

Let me encourage the reader to be aware that no problem facing humankind is completely new. Do not give up hope. The following examples might empower us to live the dream. Victory is as close to us as our doorstep. The vision for victorious 21$^{st}$ century families is within us.

## Chapter 14

## Don't Turn Out the Lights,
## The Party Is Not Over for Victorious 21st Century Families

While working one summer in Tifton, Georgia, I heard the prophetic words of the late great Gospel singer, Mahaliah Jackson, in her hit song, "Soon, I will be done with the troubles of the world."

The Bible does not state that godly families will be free from troubles of the world. Unfortunately, many people do not know how to deal with pain and suffering.

Let us delve deep into the word of God to find what certain people chosen by God did spiritually to obtain victory over the enemy, thereby unfolding God's plan for their lives. I have described below some of those examples that might encourage the reader to march on to victory:

I. SARAH. Genesis 18: 1-16; 21: 1-3: Three men appeared to Abraham. Two were angels, and the other, the Lord Himself. This is what they did:

- Abraham lifted his eyes, and focused on God
- He asked for God's FAVOR
- He and Sarah gave willingly to strangers. In so doing, they entertained the angels, unaware they had entertained God Himself.
- They demonstrated FAITH in God. Hebrews 11:11 indicates Sarah was basically a woman of faith, despite this momentary lapse. The result was that God's promise was fulfilled, despite the odds, and both Abraham, Sarah, and all who heard the good news of the fulfillment of God's promise to Sarah was filled with happiness.
In our demise, we must look up to God, and focus on Him. Additionally, we must humbly ask for His favor and

guidance in dealing with our problems marital and family relationship problems. We must do or give something good to others first, if we expect God to do the same for us.
- Let us pray and ask God to give us the strength and ability to focus on Him, and grant us His Favor as we embark on ONE PLUS ONE EQUALS ONE

II. JOSEPH. Genesis 37: 13-35; 42: 1-7; 45: 1-18, 27-28; 50: 20.

The intention of God is to bless His children. His plans and purpose for our lives are presented in the Bible. However, sometimes God chooses to reveal some of His custom-made plans to us individually within the context of scripture.

Regrettably, the enemy also sees in the spirit what blessings God has scheduled for us. Subsequently, he tries to interfere with God's plan for His children. We must stand on God's word and not allow the enemy to prevail.

Most families of the world are good-natured, with a desire to do well. Unfortunately, distractions from the enemy frustrate our efforts, and we wonder why those who are not believers in God seem to 'have it good' while those who believe, suffer. We fail to understand the existence of this spiritual conflict and thus, lead lives of depression or misery! The devil's plan of attack is usually four-fold. He will attack your mind, body, will or heart.

The devil would not disrupt what he already has. Nevertheless, he will try to frustrate the blessings God has for His children. We have the assurance that whether His blessings come right away or eventually, they will come at His time based on our faith in claiming His promises. Therefore, we must not be weary if we do not see success in the vision to victory right away.

Jacob and Joseph had good intentions for the remaining members of his family (vs. 13). However, the devil attempted to divert God's ultimate plan for Joseph. God saw the actions of the devil and used His power to guide Joseph (vs. 15). However, it appeared Joseph was unable to pick up God's signal.

God brought the knowledge of good and evil to the minds of Joseph's brothers to give them a chance to avoid evil. However, they were willing to succumb to the devil.

They conspired against Joseph, driven by anger, hatred, and jealousy. They cast Joseph into a pit. They then turned out the lights on Joseph by selling him to Ishmaelite merchants, thereby placing him on a path of doom and gloom. However, God's party for Joseph was not over.

God sent a wind of change at the peak of the story. He overruled Satan by creating famine in Canaan while providing plenty of food in Egypt. He elevated Joseph in Egypt and brought fear upon his brothers. Verses 21-22 revealed the growing conviction of sin for what his brothers did to Joseph over 20 years earlier.

Finally, God established forgiveness, love and compassion in Joseph's heart for his brothers who tried to kill him. That was a major key to Joseph's victory. How willing are you to turn your marriage and family relationship issues to Him? How willing are you to forgive your mate for his or her shortcomings?

Let us pray and ask God to teach us how to forgive, have compassion and love for our family members who have wrongfully mistreated us. This is a difficult but necessary prerequisite for VICTORY in ONE PLUS ONE EQUALS ONE.

III. Samson eventually revealed the secret of his strength to Delilah. He was a Nazarite, separated to God, from whom he derived his strength. However, he was powerless when his hair was cut off.

He tried to summon his previous strength unaware that the Lord had left him. The Philistines put out his eyes, imprisoned him in Gaza, and forced him to grind grain.

Both in past and recent history, we have read about several great men who, for one reason or another find certain women irresistible, which ultimately leads to great repercussions in their lives.

However, God's party was not over for Samson. Samson killed more men in his death than he did in his life because he repented and called upon the name of God. God is faithful and just to forgive our sins and restore us unto Him through the blood of Yahshua. Yes, we must forgive. But those who have caused us pain must also repent and seek forgiveness.

Are you willing to base your marriage and relationship on truthfulness, openness, without any hidden agendas or skeletons in your closet? Are you willing to have nothing concealed in secret, which if made public might wreck you relationship?

IV. Ruth 1: 2-4. A Jewish family left Bethlehem, which meant 'house of bread,' of Judah (praise) to Moab because of famine. It would have been better for that family to stay in Bethlehem and trust in God's ability to provide than to immigrate to Moab.

Once you read the entire story, you will find that, in fact, Bethlehem, in fact, was a land of the living. On the other hand, Moab was a land of the dead because not only did Elimelech, Mahlon, and Chilion die there; the last two did not have any children while in the land of Moab.

Sometimes, people get themselves in trouble because they do not learn to wait long enough on the promises of God. Sometimes they have no commitment in their relationship with God or have a very bad attitude. Let us look at the attitudes of the three widows in the story:

Naomi was a grieving widow, stripped of earthly joys of husband and family by divine judgment.

Orpah had a poor attitude. She was a leaving widow who chose the easiest way out of her predicament.

Ruth was a cleaving widow. She clung to Naomi in spite of her discouragements. She knew there would be hard work, poverty, and separation from home and loved ones. Nevertheless, she was committed.

Naomi insisted that her neighbors called her "Mara" because the "Almighty has dealt very bitterly with me." She went out full (husband and children) but returned empty (widow and no children). However, God's party was not over for her.

Like most believers, we sometimes backslide, but the Lord brings us back empty and usually through bitter chastening. At other times, grace, as in the case of Ruth, overrides the pit of the devil and leads us on. David, who was King of Israel, was a descendant of Ruth. Let us see how God's plan for not turning out her lights unfolded:

- It was divine grace that led Ruth to the field owned by Boaz, a wealthy relative of her late father-in-Law.
- Boaz said a prayer for Ruth that was answered by God.
- God gave Ruth favor so Boaz invited her to eat with his workers. He also granted her provisions and protection.
- Boaz had compassion on Ruth (Ch 2 Vs 1, 8-9).
- God opened the eyes of Boaz to know all about Ruth even before she met him.
- Naomi followed her inner teacher and asked Ruth to continue gleaning in the field of Boaz.
- God strengthened Ruth's loyalty. Boaz commended her (3: 10) for her loyalty, saying that her later kindness (her personal devotion to him) was better than the first (leaving home and family to be with Naomi).
- God made a way to overcome stumbling blocks of legalities and technicalities to her victory (3: 12, 13). He will always make a way where there is no way. She learned how to wait on the Lord patiently (3: 18).
- Boaz went up to the gate by divine coincidence and met a close relative next in line to marry Ruth. However, God changed that relative mind paving the way for Boaz to marry Ruth and purchase Elimelech's property to the satisfaction of all.

The beauty of the above story is that is was not one-sided. Naomi passed on her experiences and wisdom to Ruth. Ruth listened, and took the advice of the older and more experienced, Naomi. It is a two-way street.

Are you determined to hold your family together even if the winds of hunger and change blow over your relationship or are you going to be a coward and unstable minded person in times of trouble? A double-minded person is unstable in all his or her ways. Such should not expect to see the victory in ONE PLUS ONE EQUALS ONE.

V. Nehemiah. 1: 1-11; 2: 1-8. The enemies of the Jews successfully received a decree from King Artaxerxes to cease and desist work, and tear down the walls of Jerusalem. That action came to Nehemiah, an influential personality. Nehemiah gave us the following seven leadership principles that hold true today:

- Vision of a goal to be achieved
- Analysis of problem
- Determination of proper course of action
- Motivate other people to share the vision, and become actively involved
- Delegate authority and assign tasks
- Supervise work
- Check on performance until project was satisfactorily completed

When he received the news of gloom and doom, he did not turn out his lights. He knew with God's child the party was not over until God said so. He called on God to keep on the lights in favor of Jerusalem in a four part powerful prayer, which still works today –Adoration, Confession, Thanksgiving, and Supplication.

He denied himself the luxuries of the palace in order to fast, mourn, and pray. He confessed their sins as his own, and asked God to remember His word and be faithful in regathering His people, as He has been righteous in scattering them. His supplication was for favor in the sight of the King. His prayerful dependence on God was answered miraculously and unexpectedly after 3-4 months (ch. 2; 10).

How committed are you to your marriage and family to be able to deny yourself the luxuries of earthly palaces in order to fast, mourn, and pray to God for and on behalf of your families when things go wrong in your family?

Let us pray Nehemiah's prayer for what we need, and expect a miracle unexpectedly for our Vision for victorious 21$^{st}$ century families in ONE PLUS ONE EQUALS ONE.

VI.		Job. 1: 1-21; 2: 1-13; 42: 2, 7-8, 12-17.

Satan is granted permission by God to test Job by robbing him of his possessions. However, the devil was not permitted to touch his body.

Job did not turn out his lights because he knew God's party was not over until the Lord said so, and he had not heard God's voice otherwise. In Ch 1: 20-22 he stated:

"Naked came I from my mother's womb, and naked shall I return there. The Lord gave, and the Lord has taken away; blessed be the name of the Lord".

Calamity to Job's Body. Painful boils covered his entire body. His wife urged him to "curse God and die". However, he again replied rhetorically, "Shall we indeed accept well from God, and shall we not accept adversity?"

He understood God's operations (Ch. 42: 2). We also learned that God answered the prayers of certain people (Ch. 42: 7, 8). He eventually received restoration such that he had more in his latter years than his beginning. Let us pray to God to give us the patience and understanding of Job because the best is yet to come in our quest for victory over **ONE PLUS ONE EQUALS ONE**.

Are you willing to have the Faith of Job to stay hold on to your marriage, and stay with your family in times of calamity?

VII.	Mark 16: 15-18. When Yahshua (Jesus) died, Satan thought that was the end of God's plan to restore humankind to Him. However, God always has the last laugh. Yahshua (Jesus) arose from the dead, and has given us the power to keep the lights he lit over hell.

Let us pray and ask God to let our lights shine before men so they may see our good works and glorify the father in heaven. God is the source of our strength. He is a lamp unto our feet, and a light unto our path. Now that we have embarked on this journey, be assured that truly in His light, we shall see light, and thus victory in the 21$^{st}$ century.

Are you willing to take your marital vows seriously, and stay with your spouse 'until death do us part?' Are you willing to be true to yourself, obedient to your God and let Him handle the things in your relationship you cannot handle? Remember faith, acceptance, and obedience are powerful elements that set the miracles on God in action. If you can say, "Yes to all these questions, then you are ready to embark on ONE PLUS ONE EQUALS ONE!

Amen.

## Bibliography

1. Adjei, Gideon Rev. Dr., 2004, Black Ice: A Vision for Victory, Crystal Books Publisher.

2. Adjei, Gideon Dr., 2001, Darker Shades of Light, Crystal Books Publisher.

3. Advocates for youth for the Centers for Disease Control and Prevention, 2000. A Life-long dialogue: A workplace Program to Enhance Parent-Child Communication.

4. American Academy of Matrimonial Lawyers, 2005, Making Marriage Last, www.aaml.org/Marriage_Last/MarriageLastText.htm.

5. Arp, David and Claudia. M.S.S.W., 2005, You're not listening!

6. BBC, 2006. Relationships www.bbc.co.uk/relationships/singles_and_dating/techniques_flirting.shtml.

7. Boa, Kenneth, Dr., 2005. Marriage: Intimates or Inmates? (Permission granted by www.bible.org).

8. Boghart, David Holt, Jr., 1998. Spiritual Armor and Weapons, www.yahshuacenteredmail.com.

9. Brus, Karen S. C.H.E., 1996. Ten steps towards successful step parenting, Ohio State University Extension Fact Sheet HYG-5231-96, Family and Consumer Sciences, Campbell Hall 1787 Neil Avenue, Columbus, Ohio 43210.

10. Bush, George, W., President of the United States, 2003. The White House Fact Sheet: Preventing Domestic Violence. www.whitehouse.gov.

11. Calvin, Claire, 2005. Do you trust him? www.womwntodaymagazine.com/relationships/trust/html.

12. Canadian Centre for Justice Statistics, statistics Canada, 2001. Cat. No. 85-002-XPE.2001.

13. Clemenger, Bruce, 2003. Keep marriage heterosexual, Tyndale University College, Tyndale seminary, www.christianity.ca/news/social-issues/2003/09.002.hmtl.

14. Cotton, William, Dr., 2006. Houston Community College System, Town & Country Campus, Houston, Texas, personal communication.

15. Crenshaw, Alan, 2006. The spiritual meaning of marriage, part 4.

16. Crenshaw, Alan, 2006.The spiritual meaning of marriage, and the tree of life, part 2.

17. Crenshaw, Alan, 2006. The divine marriage, the spiritual meaning of sex and marriage.

18. Elam Ministries & FarsiNet Inc, 2005. God's truth about "occult": Chapter Five.

19. Forsberg, Geri, Ph.D., 2005. Learn to communicate with your partner. www.womentodaymagazine.com/relationships/communicate.html.

20. Harries, Richard, 2005. Marriage: A Christian Understanding. A pastoral letter from the bishop of Oxford, www.oxford.anglican.org.

21. Hopkinson, Natalie, 2001. "It's a family affair", The Washington Post, September 7.

22. James, Leon, Dr., University of Hawaii, 2007. Together Forever: The Unity Model of Marriage. Available on the web at: www.soc.hawaii.edu/leonj/leonj/leonpsy24/409b-g24-lecture-notes.htm.

23. McLanahan, S. & G Sandefurs (1994) Growing up with a single parent; What hurts, What helps Cambridge Mass: Harvard University Press.

24. Newsflash, 2006, Domestic Violence Widespread, Harms Health of Millions of Women Worldwide, www.who.int/.

25. Parliament of Australia, Information and Research document, 2006. www.aph.gov.au/House/Committee/laca/Famserv/Chap41.pdf.

26. Parrish, Kathleen, The Morning Call, Love does increase over time, 02/14/1999.

27. Patz, Aviva Executive Editor, 2000. Psychology Today, Predicting marital success.

28. Quillin, Patrick, Dr., 2002. Healing Secrets from the Bible.

29. Rainey, Dennis, 2005, Marriage: The three-legged race, FamilyLife.org.

30. Getting married, 2003. An Australian Government Initiative.

31. Rector, Robert E. and Melissa G. Pardue, 2004. Understanding the President's Healthy Marriage Initiative. The Heritage Foundation, Policy Research & Analysis, www.heritage.org.

32. Relationship for singles and marriage, a romantic relationship for singles and marriage looking for their perfect match, www.geocities.com/lovenrelation/relationship.hmtl.

33. Rennison, M. and W. Welchans. Intimate Partner Violence. U.S. Department of Justice, Office of Justice Programs, Bureau of Justice Statistics. May 2000, NCJ 178247, Revised 7/14/00.

34. Shamoun Sam, 2005. Muhammad and Aisha Revisited: An examination of Muhammad's marriage to a prepubescent girl and its moral implications.

35. Tha Spot, Thug Life Army Blog, 2006. Bush signs 'Violence against Women Act.'

36. Steele, David, President and Founder of LifePartnerQuest, 12 dating traps and solutions. www.lifepartnerquest.com/single/trap.htm.

37. The lover's guide, 2006. Understanding the body language, lg.loversguide.com/content/article.1.1.123.phpx; Kassian, Mary, 2005. Connect with the body language, www.womentodaymagazine.com/relationships/bodylanguage.htm

38. The United Church of Canada, 2005. Marriage, a United Church of Canada Understanding.

39. Wadley, Carma, 2000. Happily Ever After...Maybe. Deseret News, Brigham Young University.

40. Wallerstein, J. (1989) 'Daughters of divorce' American Journal of Orthopsychiatry 59: 593.

41. Wallerstein, J. & S Blakeslee (1989) Second chances: Men, women and children a decade after divorce New York.

42. Warren C. Christopher, 2005. FAQ 68. How should Christians select marriage companions, NCWUS www.nccg.org/FAQ068-marriage.hmtl.

43. www.aph.gov.au/house/committee/laca/inquiryinfam.htm.

44. www.earlymenopause.com/symptoms.htm.

45. www.LamMD.com.

46. www.menopause-online.com/pmsormenopause.html.

47. www.4woman.gov/faq/menopaus.htm.

48. www.probe.org/docs/divorce.html.